Managing Performance

Learning Made Simple

Corinne Leech

Routledge
Taylor & Francis Group

LONDON AND NEW YORK

T0384868

First published 2007 by Butterworth-Heinemann
Published 2015 by Routledge
2 Park Square, Milton Park, Abingdon, Oxon, OX14 4RN
711 Third Avenue, New York, NY 10017

Routledge is an imprint of the Taylor & Francis Group, an informa business

Notice
No responsibility is assumed by the publisher for any injury and/or damage to
persons or property as a matter of products liability, negligence or otherwise, or from
any use or operation of any methods, products, instructions or ideas contained in the
material herein.

British Library Cataloguing in Publication Data
A catalogue record for this book is available from the British Library.

Library of Congress Cataloguing in Publication Data
A catalogue record for this book is available
from the Library of Congress.

ISBN: 978-0-7506-8407-1

Edited and typeset by P.K. McBride

Cartoons by John Leech

Icons designed by Sarah Ward © 1994

Contents

What is performance management?

Successful organisations get the best from their employees by having:

◆ A process which makes sure everyone has objectives that contribute towards the organisation's goals.

◆ Managers with the skills to support people to perform well.

Both are equally important. An organisation which is good at performance management supports its people to achieve the organisation's goals.

What can go wrong?

Effective performance management is a challenge for a whole variety of reasons.

What can go wrong?

With the process …	With the people …
Business plan objectives not cascaded down	No time to do it
No guidance in the process for setting individual objectives	Don't understand the process
Degenerates into a form-filling exercise	See it as a form-filling exercise
Too complicated	Avoid managing poor performance
Not communicated	Lack the skills to review performance

Confidence in the process disappears. Managers do their own thing – or do nothing at all. An opportunity, which can bring benefits to everyone, is lost.

Getting it right

As a line manager you need to put performance management at the heart of working with your team. It should be driving what your team is doing on a daily basis. In some organisations this may be in spite of the process rather than because of it.

This book explores the behaviours needed to manage performance as well as the processes. It will encourage you to reflect on the working environment you create by the nature of your management style. Getting people management right is often a far greater challenge than following guidelines on what should be done, by when, to keep the organisation's system on track.

If your role is to develop a performance management system, pay equal attention to developing:

◆ The process.

◆ The people.

You will find actions specific to developing a system throughout the book.

The route through the chapters

Chapter 1: The bigger picture

You can't manage performance effectively without understanding how you and your team fit into the wider picture. Therefore this is the place to start.

Chapter 2: The human dimension

Managing performance is as much about people as it is about processes. In a nutshell, a good people manager understands, or at least considers, what makes people tick. This chapter explores some of the factors which affect how people perform at work. Then it's over to you to consider your behaviour and the impact it has on others.

Chapter 3: The toolkit

Dissect any performance management system and you are likely to find a number of standard components. This chapter looks at them and explores how each one is designed to add value to the overall process. You are likely to find that some you'll be familiar with; others will be new. Few performance management systems use them all.

Chapter 4: The skills

So what exactly do you need to do? We look at a range of skills which are essential to make the process work. How do you assess performance, give constructive feedback and manage those one-to-one meetings? Chapter 4 examines the various skills involved and gives you practical checklists against which to assess your performance.

Chapter 5: The team culture

Back to the foundations of effective performance management. This chapter is about using the theories explored in Chapter 2 to create a working environment in which people want to perform. There are many things you won't be able to influence at work; but the culture within your team isn't one of them!

Chapter 6: Poor performance

This chapter explores how to address the problem of underperformance through a combination of reviewing your behaviour and using organisational processes. It may be the first chapter you turn to. If so, we suggest you use it in conjunction with the *Managing performance: review.*

Managing performance: review

Use this to reflect on your performance and check you're doing what's needed to achieve your potential when managing performance.

 Key point

Managing performance is about managing people, within the framework of a process, to achieve the organisation's goals.

1 The bigger picture

Understanding the bigger picture

Managing performance is about managing people within the framework of a process, to achieve the organisation's goals

So, what is the process that links the organisational goals to an individual? This chapter gives an overview of where managing performance fits into how organisations operate and survive. In practice, the way organisations operate is very similar across the private, public and not-for-profit sectors. They all have to start by planning:

1   Where they are going.

2   How they are going to get there.

Although the principle is simple, in reality, steering an organisation successfully is exceedingly challenging. We live in a world where change is just about the only constant you can rely on. Making a wrong decision, or failing to see what's happening round the next corner, can have dire consequences on an organisation's fortunes or a chief executive's career.

But planning alone isn't going to ensure success. The plan has to be cascaded through the organisation so that:

◆   Everyone understands the part they have to play, and

◆   Their performance can be managed.

This chapter looks at:

◆   Why organisations have to evolve.

◆   How they meet the challenges.

◆   How they try to achieve alignment (i.e. everyone working to achieve the organisation's goals).

By the end you'll be able to ask the right questions to understand exactly how you, and your team, fit in to the bigger picture in your organisation.

He who asks may be a fool for five minutes but he who does not remains a fool forever.

Chinese proverb

Why organisations have to evolve

How many organisations do you know that have stayed the same over the last ten, or even five years? The chances are you'd be hard pressed to name any. Outsourcing, downsizing, restructuring, takeovers have become the language of the workplace. If organisations don't evolve they simply don't survive.

What's driving evolution?

In a nutshell, there are three driving forces:

1 The mantra of 'continuous improvement'

Any organisation exists to meet the needs of its customers. Continuous improvement is a process which has evolved out of the quality revolution which began in the 1940s. Its aim is to keep the customer satisfied and to continually improve the services and products offered. This means organisations have to continually search for ways of improving. Inevitably this means change.

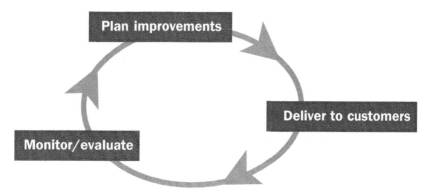

Figure 1.1 Continuous improvement cycle

2 The business case

The business case often drives the need for change. In the private sector it's about increasing profitability. In the public and the not-for-profit sectors it's about best value. Everything has a cost attached and everywhere organisations are looking to reduce costs, justify costs, get value for money.

What was the quality revolution?

Japan applied the concept of quality to build its manufacturing capacity following the Second World War. Initially it focussed on 'quality control', i.e. a rigorous process for checking products met exacting standards. It developed into 'quality assurance' which included looking at the standard of all the inputs as well as checking the products. The concept is now widely applied in the West, and has evolved into 'Total Quality Management'. This is a management approach that puts meeting customer expectations at the heart of everything. ISO 9000 and the European Excellence Model are examples of organisations getting external accreditation for demonstrating they have management systems which will meet, or even exceed, customer expectations.

 A business case is a justification to commit resources to a project. It will usually include: objectives, benefits, option appraisal, risk assessment and costings.

3 Technology

Speed of change in technology is ever-increasing. For those involved in the computing industry it is often the case that products are being superseded as soon as they hit the shelves.

But the impact of these changes are felt in all organisations.

Reducing labour costs

Joiners making stud walls used to accurately measure the timber, cut it squarely then chop and chisel joints to pin and screw together to construct the wall framework. Technology has provided portable bench saws to cut accurately and squarely first time, nail guns which allow one man to hold and secure joints and what was a day's work can now be done in a couple of hours with less waste.

Change has become the law of life. But often people find coping with it difficult. Inevitably it will have an impact on managing performance as people tend to find the uncertainty of change demotivating. It's human nature.

But is it sometimes change for change's sake?

It's easy to suspect.

Research by the Chartered Management Institute (2001) found that 60% of the 5000 managers interviewed had undergone a major restructuring each year for the past five years.

People can so easily become jaded by having to implement continual change. Change itself becomes the chief suspect when, in many cases, it's the nature, method and manner of implementation which is at fault. If you accept the three driving forces for evolution, change is what's going to happen anyway. What's important is that the change is understood and communicated.

Organisations have to evolve to survive. Therefore performance has to be managed within a constantly changing environment. It can't be ignored or avoided. However its effects can be mitigated if the change is understood and communicated.

Activity

Find out:

- ❖ What have the main changes been in your organisation in the last two years?
- ❖ What has driven the changes?
- ❖ What are the changes which are likely to happen in the next two years?
- ❖ What's driving them?

How do you view changes? Your attitude will have a major impact on how you communicate them to your team, which in turn will impact on their attitudes and motivation.

If you find change a challenge, then the Learning Made Simple book on Change will help you to put what's happening into perspective.

Meeting the challenges

Organisations need to:

1   Know where they are heading

2   Have a strategy (i.e. a plan) for getting there

3   Take their people with them.

It's a continuous process because at any stage they have to be ready to adapt to changing circumstances. A performance management system will provide the vehicle to take the people with them. But creating or implementing any system demands an understanding of the first two steps.

Where are we going?

Alice: Which way should I go?

Cat: That depends on where you're going.

Alice: I don't know where I'm going!

Cat: Then it doesn't matter which way you go!

Through the Looking Glass, Lewis Carroll, 1872

Organisations have to know where they want to get to. Maintaining the 'status quo' isn't an option, and without a clear direction they are likely to end up in trouble. It involves planning a journey into the future. Where does the organisation want to be in two or five years' time?

Often it's captured in terms of a vision or mission statement, e.g.

'To be Britain's best value retailer exceeding customers needs. Always! www.ASDA.co.uk November 2006

Many organisations also have a set of values which aim to guide the behaviour of employees from the Chief Executive to front-line staff.

ASDA values

Respect for the individual

Strive for excellence

Service to our customers

In some organisations, assessment of behaviour against values is incorporated into the performance management system.

Miss one development cycle and you are seriously hurt. Miss two and you are mortally wounded.

Scott G McNealy, Chairman, President, CEO, Sun Microsytems

Strategic aims and objectives

More detail of an organisation's direction is given in the strategic aims or objectives. These high-level objectives define what the mission might look like in practice. Often you'll find strategic aims are about:

Growth: e.g. increase market share by 5%

Markets: e.g. expand into another region

Services: e.g. develop services for older people.

Every organisation needs a clear sense of direction.

Activity

Where is your organisation heading? Find out its:

❖ Mission, vision or goals. You may also find it has values which set the framework for the sorts of behaviours the organisation wants to embody.

❖ Strategic objectives.

If you work for a big, or even a global, organisation it may be easier to find them out for your part of the organisation, e.g. your group or division.

Good places to start looking are in the Annual Accounts or website.

The use of values as a performance tool is explored in Chapter 3.

Setting the strategy

Knowing where you want to get to is the first step. Organisations then need a strategy for getting there. It involves:

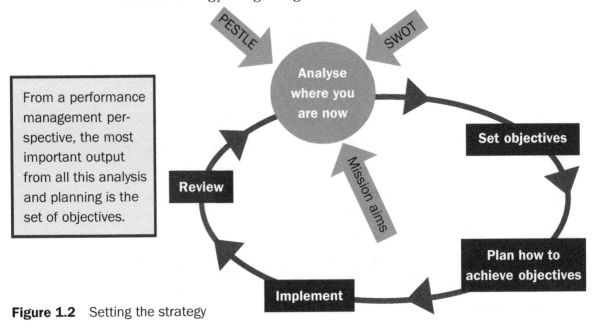

> From a performance management perspective, the most important output from all this analysis and planning is the set of objectives.

Figure 1.2 Setting the strategy

A similar process takes place at all levels within an organisation and marks the start of the continuous improvement cycle. At the high level it tends to be referred to as strategy, at the department or service level it may simply be called planning.

PESTLE and SWOT

A PESTLE analysis is a systematic exploration of all external factors which could have a potential impact. It can take place an organisational, business unit or individual service level. Factors considered are: Political, Economic, Social, Technological, Legal, Environmental.

There are plenty of examples of how PESTLE factors affect strategies within organisations. For example, the 'green' agenda, the price of fuel, technological advances and equal opportunities legislation.

A SWOT analysis involves considering:

◆ Internal **Strengths** and **Weaknesses** (skills, resources, expertise)

◆ External **Opportunities** and **Threats** (new markets, competitors, results of a PESTLE analysis)

 PESTLE and SWOT analysis can take place at all levels in an organisation, e.g. from Board to team level. Information collection should always be an ongoing activity. Keep a log of factors as they emerge so you have the information ready.

Influencing strategy in practice

Rising awareness of obesity in the population is a social issue which is impacting on the strategies of organisations in a number of areas. For example:

◆ School meal providers are changing their menus.

◆ Fast food outlets are adapting their menus.

◆ Convenience food producers are minimising their use of hydrogenated fats.

◆ Advertising bans are causing confectionery producers to rethink their marketing strategies.

◆ Businesses with a 'healthy food' image are facing increasing demands for their products.

Is it the right direction?

There are no guarantees. You only have to look at the High Street to find big name brands that either temporarily or permanently chose the wrong direction.

Alignment is the key

Figure 1.3 Aligning the organisation

This is the ideal for any organisation – every person's output contributing to achieving the strategic objectives. It's called alignment. Everybody needs to be pulling in the same direction to ensure this.

The team improvised admirably and overcame the sudden power cut which had threatened the deadline.

Activities

1 Get to know your organisation

What is the business planning cycle for your organisation? When are budget plans made and budgets set? How does this fit in with the policies and procedures around managing performance, e.g. is there a time set for annual appraisals?

Does it all make sense? If it's not obvious, ask your manager how it works. It's difficult to manage performance if you can't see how it fits in to the bigger picture.

2 Developing a performance management system

When developing a performance management system, the first step is to find out:

❖ When the business planning cycle is within your organisation.

❖ When the organisational objectives for the year are established so they can inform the performance management process. This will be a key date as it can signal the start of the annual performance objective setting cycle.

❖ When you need performance to be reviewed so it can contribute towards next year's planning cycle.

Draw up a calendar so you can begin to see when key performance management activities should take place.

Then consult. Ask managers across the organisation for their views. You must get buy-in to the process from the beginning.

Achieving alignment

Achieving alignment has to start at the top, from the organisations strategic objectives. The organisation has to:

1 Look at what it wants to achieve (its strategic objectives), and

2 Cascade relevant objectives to each operating area.

Figure 1.4 Cascading objectives

The trick is to ensure that sum of the objectives cascaded will achieve the organisation's aims.

unit A objectives + unit B objectives + unit C objectives = what the organisation aims to achieve.

And so the process continues. Down through the organisation until every employee has their personal work objectives which, when collectively achieved, will mean the organisation achieves its goals.

If the organisation is large, or even global, the cascading process will go through several more levels than a small organisation. However, the principle is the same for every organisation.

Key point

Other names for strategic objectives include: business goals, organisational aims, business objectives, strategic aims. They all serve the same purpose: setting the direction for the organisation.

Objectives are the key

The cascading of objectives down the organisation drives the process of performance management. No matter the size or type of organisation, the end result should be that everyone has individual work objectives that can be traced up to its strategic objectives.

Strategic objectives	A furniture company on the south coast has a strategic objective to expand into mainland Europe
Business plan objectives	A business plan objective in the first year was to set up a distribution network in three capital cities

down through the hierarchy

Individual work objectives	The logistics manager had a work objective to negotiate a distribution deal with an international haulage firm within the next three months

The example is simplistic. For some roles, especially support roles or roles which are repetitive task-based, the links can seem more difficult to make. What's important is that there is a clear link of individual objectives to the organisation's goals.

Pitfalls

Alignment of objectives in many organisations can be far from perfect for a variety of reasons.

Activity

Below is a list of common pitfalls. Do any apply to your organisation?

❖ Little, or no attempt is made to create a link between the higher-level objectives and individual work objectives.

❖ Staff aren't made aware of the higher-level objectives.

❖ The planning cycle is out of sync with the annual performance reviews/ appraisals round.

❖ Managers and/or other staff aren't trained to understand the process.

If you can identify one or more of the pitfalls in your organisation, it doesn't mean that it's impossible to manage performance. It does mean that the organisation isn't going to gain the benefits that alignment can bring.

Checklist

- ◆ Make sure annual performance reviews coincide with the start of the implementation of the annual business plan.

- ◆ Provide clear guidance and training to make the links.

- ◆ Involve managers and other staff when developing a system.

Take note

The only way to achieve alignment is for every employee to have work objectives which contribute to the wider organisational objectives.

This vertical cascade of objectives to align the organisation is only part of the overall performance management process. It has to link into the performance management cycle.

The performance management cycle

The performance management cycle is the process by which a manager manages the performance of another member of staff. The cycle is simple. It consists of meetings in which performance is reviewed and planned. Work is then carried out and another meeting is held to review and plan performance. And so the cycle continues.

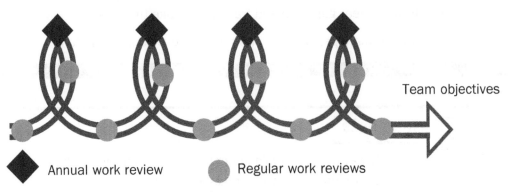

Figure 1.5   The performance management cycle

Linking into the alignment of objectives

The previous section focused on the importance of cascading business objectives down to an individual level. The intersection between the vertical cascade and the performance management cycle takes place annually. It's a formal meeting, commonly referred to as an 'appraisal' or annual review. For example:

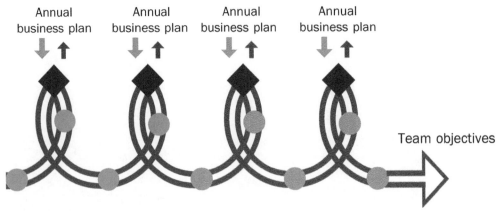

Figure 1.6   A performance management system

Note the smaller arrows taking feedback upwards. The system should allow the upward flow of feedback which can be incorporated into the next round of business planning.

Of course, organisations vary. Some may have longer term 'rolling' business plans. But whatever the situation the principle is the same. There has to be a point at which the wider organisational plans intersect with the ongoing process of performance management with individual staff.

A typical annual review meeting

The meeting will usually have three main parts:

◆ Looking backwards – reviewing or appraising performance during the year.

◆ Looking forwards – performance planning for the forthcoming year (i.e. setting objectives for the forthcoming year, often with accompanying performance measures and broken down into shorter-term targets).

◆ Development planning – identifying what skills and knowledge are needed to ensure the work objectives can be achieved and how they will be met.

Outcomes are recorded on standardised documentation and filed to form a permanent record of performance.

 Review or appraisal of performance is only part of the performance management process. Planning is a key element.

Regular review meetings

These are essential. Somewhere between every six weeks and three months there needs to be a conversation which reviews progress against the objectives or targets set.

 The skills of managing one-to-one meetings are explored in Chapter 4.

Research by the Industrial Society found that the most common purpose of reviews was to improve motivation, with eight out of ten organisations listing this as one of the main purposes. More than half of organisations also state that they aim to enhance career development and promote productivity.

Managing Performance, no 86, The Industrial Society, August 2001

As the research highlights, regular review meetings can serve a number of purposes. This is why the 'people' skills of a manager are so important to ensure that the best possible outcomes are achieved.

Summary

◆   Managing performance is about combining the people dimension with an organisational process.

◆   To manage performance you need to know how you and your team fit into the wider organisation. Find the answers to these questions:

   ❖   What changes are happening now and why?

   ❖   What changes are likely to happen in the future; what's driving them?

   ❖   What your organisation trying to achieve? What are its objectives?

   ❖   Does it have values? If so, how do they impact on decisions?

   ❖   How do the different parts of the organisation fit together? How is it aligned? Where do you fit in?

◆   A performance management system includes:

   ❖   The way the wider organisational objectives are cascaded down to the individual level

   ❖   The performance management cycle, i.e. the process by which individual managers manage performance.

2 The human dimension

Motivation

Research studies show that the greatest factor influencing motivation at work is often the line manager.

Understanding what makes people tick is key to managing performance. That doesn't mean a degree in psychology; just the ability to recognise what's likely to motivate people to perform well. As a general rule, people who perform well at work do so because something, or someone, has caused them to want to. So, how can you impact on this 'want' factor? There are three fundamental principles.

1 You *can't* control a person's level of motivation.

2 You *can* influence it.

3 One of the biggest factors influencing your team's level of motivation is likely to be you.

However tempting it may be, it's a non-starter to tell someone to 'be happy' or 'be more enthusiastic'. The same applies to telling someone to 'get motivated'. People aren't like puppets with strings; you can't control how they behave – but you can create an environment in which people are likely to feel motivated to perform well.

 Motivation is the inner drive which makes us want to do things. Every manager needs to ask, 'How can I create an environment in which people feel motivated?'

This chapter explores some of the theories which explain:

◆ Why you can't control someone else's motivation.

◆ The psychology behind getting the best out of your team.

◆ The impact your behaviour has on people around you.

◆ How to increase your awareness of this impact.

If you're not already familiar with the theories, you will probably find that they confirm aspects of human behaviour that you know instinctively. They also lay the foundations for explaining why the practical suggestions for creating an environment which is motivating, explored in Chapter 5, actually work.

Motivation is about meeting needs

Human beings have needs. At the most basic level, if we have a need for water (i.e. we're thirsty) we will usually take immediate action to meet that need – by getting a drink. Needs are powerful motivators.

Maslow's hierarchy of needs

In the 1960s Abraham Maslow, a psychologist, identified five main types of need. He used a hierarchy to represent his idea that people tended to focus on lower level of needs i.e. their physiological needs before satisfying needs towards the top of the hierarchy.

Need for personal fulfilment

Need to feel good about yourself

Need for social interaction

Need to feel secure

Meeting basic physiological needs, e.g. for food and warmth

Figure 2.1 Maslow's hierarchy of needs

Activity

We've already given the example of getting a drink to satisfy a need for water. Thinking about the workplace, what could be offered which would go some way towards meeting each of level in Maslow's hierarchy?

You may have thought of things like:

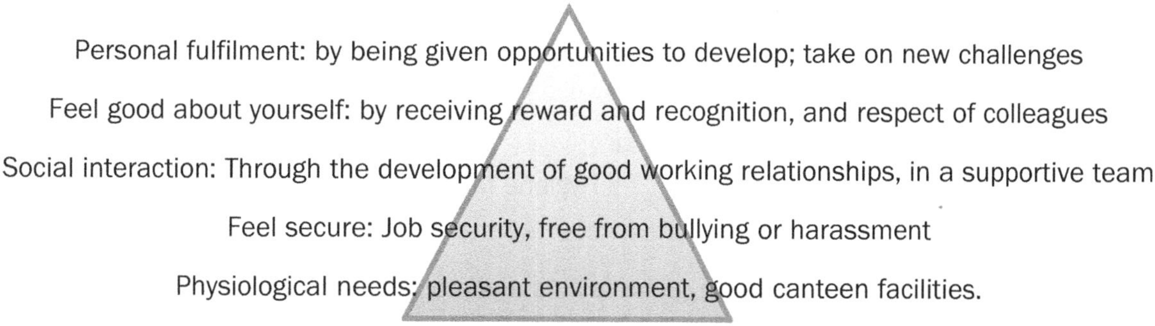

Personal fulfilment: by being given opportunities to develop; take on new challenges

Feel good about yourself: by receiving reward and recognition, and respect of colleagues

Social interaction: Through the development of good working relationships, in a supportive team

Feel secure: Job security, free from bullying or harassment

Physiological needs: pleasant environment, good canteen facilities.

Factors that affect motivation are sometimes referred to as 'intrinsic' and 'extrinsic'. Extrinsic factors are things which other people control, e.g. reward, recognition, job security. Intrinsic factors are equivalent to Maslow's 'personal fulfilment' needs i.e. 'inner factors'.

Although Maslow's theory can explain a lot, it can be difficult to see the link between a good canteen and motivation to perform well. For that we have to look to Fredrick Herzberg, a clinical psychologist, for a theory that more appropriately explains behaviour in the workplace.

Herzberg's theory

Herzberg distinguished between:

◆ Hygiene factors, which need to be satisfied if people are to avoid become jaded, irritated or dissatisfied with their lot.

◆ Motivators – factors which ignite a drive to perform well.

Examples of hygiene factors include a decent environment, fairness in the implementation of policies, confidence in management and job security. These factors need to be satisfied to avoid having a detrimental effect on performance.

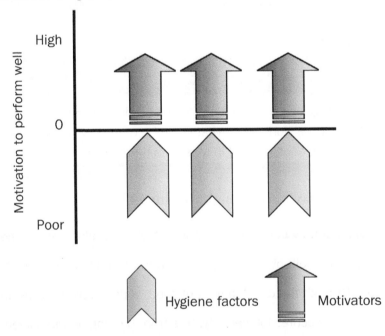

Figure 2.2 The effect of Herzberg's hygiene factors and motivators on performance

However, in order to ignite a drive to perform well, Herzberg believed we need to look at the motivators. These include things like:

◆ Recognition for work done

◆ Personal fulfilment

◆ A sense of achievement from doing the job

◆ Opportunities to advance career.

Activity

Can you think of an example where you have worked in a situation where the hygiene factors weren't met but you were still very motivated to perform well?

In some situations, good leadership, team spirit or personal determination can overcome the hygiene factors so they don't affect performance. It's certainly not impossible – but having to overcome these factors can make managing performance much harder.

Control over the motivators

Most managers have more control over the motivators than satisfiers. If the food in the canteen is bad or the building is grim there is often little you can do other than put forward your team members' perspectives to whoever has the authority to make changes. However, many of the motivators will be within your control. For example, by:

◆ Encouraging development

◆ Recognising achievements

◆ Developing trust.

 See Chapter 5 for examples of using these strategies in practice.

The theories in practice

Activity

Consider the following description of a line manager.

Dave's good. He acknowledges when a job's difficult and recognises when we hit the targets and do it well. We know it's not in his remit to give bonuses or anything like that but he listens when the pressure's on and is just generally supportive. He'll either coach us himself or make sure we get the right training course when something changes and we need new skills. The whole team celebrates when we get a big order out and if anything goes wrong we can talk openly about what happened – no one's looking for a scapegoat.

Distribution team member

❖ In Maslow's terms, what needs is Dave meeting in his team?

❖ Now in Herzberg's, what motivators is Dave using?

What's important to recognise when managing performance is that:

◆ People will tend to perform well when they are generally satisfied with the organisation, have work they find interesting or enjoy, have good working relationships and are recognised and rewarded for the effort they put it.

◆ People have similar, but not identical, needs, particularly at the top of Maslow's hierarchy. For example, one person may find being given additional responsibility or taking on a new challenge as very motivating; another might reject the idea as being simply more hassle.

Motivation is about expectations

Another approach to explaining motivation is to explore how people are motivated to do things because they expect certain results from their actions. For example:

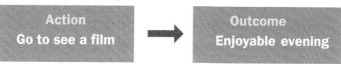

Expectancy theory

In the 1960s Victor Vroom used this basic principle to develop a model to explain how people are motivated at work.

He introduced two terms:

◆ Valence = How much satisfaction you'll get from a particular outcome

◆ Expectancy = how likely it is that you'll get the results

Motivation to do something is a product of expectancy and valence.

Expectancy	×	**Valence**	=	**Motivation**
Heard it's a really good film – just what I like		I always enjoy a good film		Motivated to go
E = 1	×	**V = 1**		

In this example:

$E \times V = M$
$1 \times 1 = 1$

But suppose you had heard it was a really bad film. Your expectancy that you'll enjoy the film will plummet and therefore the strength of the driving force to go to the cinema could totally disappear.

$E \times V = M$
$0 \times 1 = 0$

 Vroom's theory is that motivation results from recognising the potential benefits of doing something **and** knowing you have a good chance of realising them.

23

Expectancy theory in the workplace

Vroom recognised that there could be two levels of outcome:

◆ First-level outcomes which are the direct result of effort put in (i.e. work objectives met or exceeded).

◆ Second-level outcomes which link directly to satisfaction.

Although the first level outcome may not itself provide personal benefits, knowledge that there is a high likelihood of it leading to a second level outcome should provide the necessary motivation.

So the process would look like this:

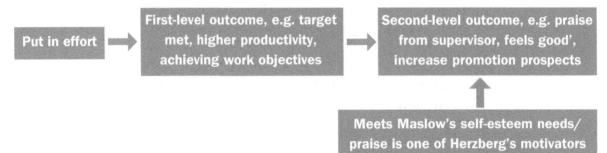

Expectancy theory in practice

Expectancy theory highlights that for people to be motivated they must:

◆ Know what the first-level outcome is.

◆ Be confident that there will be a second-level outcome which they will value.

◆ See the link between the first and second-level outcomes.

Activity

Try to identify an occasion when you were set a task or project. What were the first-level outcomes? What do you feel were the second-level outcomes that you expected? Did you make the link between the first and second-level outcomes (consciously or, with hindsight, unconsciously)?

Expectancy theory offers valuable lessons for managing performance:

◆ Make sure first-level outcomes (often set in the form of objectives) are specific and understood.

- Find out what second-level outcomes staff find motivating. It's no use deciding that the personal satisfaction gained from a new challenge will motivate someone if they are going through a period in their life where any new challenge equates with extra hassle. Talk to your team – asking them what they like and don't like about the job can give powerful insights into what motivates them.

- Make sure expectations around the second-level outcomes are met. Promises have to be kept, expectations have to be realised. In Vroom's terms, if 'expectancy' is reduced so will the motivation.

Making the link between heightened performance and personal benefits can positively influence the motivation level of people in your team.

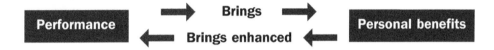

Later chapters explore the practicalities of applying the theories of motivation. For example, by setting SMART objectives, making time to listen, recognising achievements, encouraging development and developing trust.

But central to being able to do all these things is to have an awareness of the impact your behaviour has generally on the people around you. The remaining sections in this chapter explore what that means in practice.

Figure 2.3 Creating the conditions to motivate

Notice the impact of your behaviour

Whether you feel motivation is 'needs led' or 'expectations led', it is a simple fact that your behaviour (what you say and do), will influence the performance of your team.

At its most basic level, you probably will have noticed that when you're in a good mood it impacts on the people around you. They respond to the 'positive vibes' you emit. You feel good, you communicate it, it's infectious and people around you respond in a similar vein. The same principle works with everyone; the operator at the check-out desk of a supermarket, casual acquaintances, people that you're close to.

The best way to cheer yourself up is to cheer everybody else up.

Mark Twain

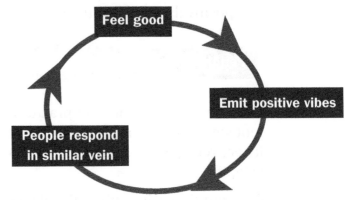

Although most people recognise this, many find it more difficult to take the next step of deciding to actively control their own behaviour to influence the people around them. It's not easy to change your attitude, especially if you are surrounded by people who are generally down beat about things.

Since the late 1990s a branch of psychology has grown which focuses on positive aspects of human behaviour. At an organisational level it promotes the importance of the creation of positive environments to allow people to flourish. At an individual level it extols the capacity of the individual to choose their outlook and attitude. In other words you have a choice over whether you see the glass as being half empty or half full; choose to see it half full and you'll exude the positive emotions which will have a positive impact on the people around you.

Taking control

It can be difficult to break into a positive cycle. Feeling low, pressures, problems, negative people around you; they all make it difficult. There's no easy answer. However, taking the first step of recognising that your behaviour affects the people around and then acknowledging that you and only you are responsibile for the way you come across to other people is crucial. Consider this scenario.

Choosing a negative attitude

Chris is Head of Personnel in an organisation due to launch a staff survey. There have been many rounds of consultation to develop the questions. Jessica, a personnel officer who is in Chris's team and has had the most hands-on input into the finalising the questions, contacts Chris to say she's just had a e-mail from health and safety asking for two new questions to be inserted. Chris knows from previous experience that they are just pointless information-gathering which will add to the survey's length and risk alienating respondents. He tells Jessica why they can't be used, sending a clear message of his irritation that people really don't think before making requests. At lunchtime Jessica tells her colleague that she feels like piggy-in-the-middle. She really doesn't care what questions are in as long as everyone is happy and don't come back at her if they're not.

Chris's attitude successfully dampened Jessica's spirits, calling on her to have to fight hard to stay enthusiastic and committed about the project. Supposing Chris had risen above his initial reaction, hidden his irritation, and responded in an upbeat fashion. For example:

An alternative approach

'You always get the last minute suggestions. Don't worry about it. Go back and check exactly why they want the questions and see if there's another way of getting the information. They may find that the information is already in the training records. Overall I think it's looking really good, starting to take shape nicely. What are your plans for piloting?'

The impact on Jessica is likely to be very different. Here's a line manager who offers helpful suggestions, reassurance and shows interest in the project.

Do you positively or negatively influence the motivation of the people around you? How do you come across to people?

❖ Is your glass generally half empty or half full?

❖ Do you verbalise the positives to others, or do you assume that they'll they will see them?

❖ How do you react when someone:

- Has to tell you 'bad news'?

- Asks you a favour?

Now ask a friend, colleague, partner or someone in your team for their perception. It needs to be someone who knows you well and will be honest.

Asking someone else for their perception of your behaviour can be a brave step to take. However, it often results in useful feedback. Of course, you have to be ready to receive that feedback which can require a shift in mindset.

 ## Key points

You can't motivate other people but your behaviour will influence how motivated they are.

By taking control of your own behaviour you can influence the way people around you behave.

Be more aware of your behaviour

If you want to proactively influence others you have to increase awareness of your behaviour and how it impacts on others. The more you become aware of your own behaviour:

◆ The greater degree of control you will have over it, and

◆ The more you will be able to influence the behaviour of others and, in turn, their level of motivation to perform.

The good news is that increasing awareness of your behaviour is straightforward. But it does take a little time and involves reflecting and learning from things that have happened.

 His work on emotional intelligence has led Daniel Goleman to identify self-awareness as a key competence relating to success in the workplace at a managerial level. Self-awareness includes the ability to recognise your emotions and their effects and know your strengths and limitations.

How people learn

So how do you do it? First you need to have some awareness of how people learn.

Any type of learning takes brain activity. To learn we have to process information and make sense of it. The way most people learn is shown by a 'learning cycle', developed by the psychologist David Kolb in the late 1970s. It highlights that learning involves thinking as well as doing.

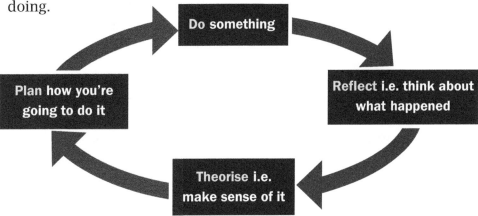

The stages of the learning cycle may happen very quickly, without you being conscious of the thought process. For example:

Do something: Cut finger with sharp knife

Think: That hurt

Work out why: That's the wrong way to hold a knife

Plan: Will hold it differently next time

As adults we seem to be less able to learn from experience. We don't bother to reflect on things that happen; instead it's often either straight on to the next activity due to the pressure of work or 'shutdown and chill-out' in an effort to gain space from the day's frantic activity.

Using the learning cycle to increase awareness

Increasing awareness of your behaviour involves *thinking*.

Thinking is the hardest work there is, which is the probably the reason so few engage in it.

Henry Ford

Reflecting and learning

Karen is a team leader in a call centre. Targets are demanding and her team is newly appointed. After one particularly bad Friday she analysed what had actually gone wrong. She was darting between problems as they cropped up with a 'headless chicken' approach which had the knock-on effect of unsettling the whole team. It would be better to prioritise tasks and complete them. On Monday morning she drew up a list of what she had to get through, decided what was most important, and scheduled time to do it. Monday wasn't a perfect day but it was a lot better than Friday.

Spencer was in a meeting. He felt that his points were being ignored and he wasn't being listened to. He left the meeting feeling very frustrated. On reflection he recognised that he hadn't read through the relevant documents. When he did he realised that his contributions must have seemed ill informed. He recognised he had a choice; either prepare thoroughly or keep quiet.

Both Karen and Spencer are learning through the process:

1   They interact with someone.

2   They think about it.

3   They make sense of it.

Then using the results of this increased awareness:

4   They plan how to do it next time.

5   They try out their plan...and so the circle goes on.

Everyone is skilled at using the process because it's how we learn throughout our lives. What often happens is that the demands of daily living mean it can be difficult to put the time aside to do it - we get out of the habit.

What's important to recognise is that the process of developing greater awareness of behaviour can take only a couple of minutes of 'quality' thinking time.

Activity

1   Getting into the habit of reflecting on what happens is likely to be the most challenging part of the exercise. You may find it helpful to be structured in your approach until it becomes a normal part of your daily routine. For example:

❖   Set aside a certain time of the day for reflection, e.g. part of a daily commute.

❖   End the day with 5 minutes of 'thinking time'. Consider:

◆   What went well?

◆   What went not so well?

◆   What was my attitude like?

◆   Is there anything I could learn from the behaviour of those around me?

2   Set up an 'review log' with a structured proforma with headings such as: What happened? What are the learning points? How would I approach it next time? Keep it simple though and don't feel you have to slavishly complete it every day. Although more time-consuming, this can provide an invaluable evidence of continued professional development and a basis for discussion with a mentor, tutor, or your own line manager.

Make time to think about how you behave and the impact it has on people around you. Increasing awareness of your behaviour can help you to influence the behaviour of people around you.

Check your attitude

Do you really feel that it's your responsibility to create an environment which people will find motivating to work in? Your response will probably depend on your attitude to managing people generally.

In his book, *The Human Side of Enterprise* (1960), Douglas McGregor categorised managers as having either 'Theory X' or 'Theory Y' attitudes towards people at work.

Activity

Consider the following pairs of statements and decide which one most accurately reflects your attitude.

1   The average person only works because they have to. They would avoid it if they could.

   Generally people enjoy working. It forms an important part of their lives.

2   The average person can't be trusted. They will shirk working if possible and therefore need to be closely supervised.

   Most people tend to work best when they are trusted to get on with things.

3   Generally people have to be coerced, bribed or threatened to really put some effort in at work.

   Most people will work willing when they get fulfilment or recognition for doing a job.

4   Most people have to be told what to do and be closely monitored otherwise the chances are things will go wrong.

   Given the right briefing and resources most people will do a good job.

If you lean towards the first statement of each pair, you have a tendency towards a 'Theory X' attitude to people management. It means that you feel comfortable with an authoritarian style, preferring to tell people what to do rather than risk them using their own initiative. The second statement of each pair is typical of a 'Theory Y' approach to managing. You recognise that people are usually willing to work well, given the right environment and management.

 A manager who adopts a 'Theory Y' attitude to management will find it easier to create an environment in which staff feel motivated than a manager who adopts a 'Theory X' approach. If you have tendencies towards Theory X then you are likely to find performance management more difficult.

Getting ahead

Increasingly it is being recognised that the most successful people in the workplace or those who have good people skills. As well as being self-aware they have an ability to build good working relationships based on an understanding of 'what makes people tick'. Sometimes they're referred to as the soft skills of management. For many people they can present a challenge, but for anyone who wants to get on in the workplace, it's a challenge worth pursuing.

Summary

◆ Key to managing performance is understanding what makes people tick.

◆ Good performance results from being motivated.

◆ You can't control a person's level of motivation, but a manager can create an environment in which people feel motivated.

◆ Meeting personal needs is a powerful motivator.

◆ Getting personal benefits from doing something also fuels our motivation to do it.

◆ A manager's behaviour has a major impact on a team's motivation level depending on whether it helps or hinders:

  ◆ Meeting personal needs

  ◆ Bringing personal benefits.

◆ Increase awareness of your own behaviour and the impact it has on others.

◆ Check your attitude!

3 The tool kit

The performance management toolkit

There are plenty of tools in the performance management toolkit. But like any tools:

◆ They have to be relevant to the job you're trying to do

◆ They are only as good as the skills of the people using them.

Organisations should select the tools which best fit their planning processes and culture. For example, 360-degree feedback is best introduced in organisations where there is a relatively high degree of openness and trust. A formal balanced scorecard demands a higher level of co-ordination across the organisation than a simple annual appraisal meeting.

Understanding the process that your organisation has adopted, and the benefits each component part can bring, is important:

◆ To maximise its usefulness

◆ To sell the benefits of the process to the people you manage.

If you are developing a process for your organisation then it pays to get an overview of the potential tools available. Then it's about selecting the right ones for your organisation – ones which will help optimise performance and align outputs with the organisation's objectives.

Beware!

Tools and processes can create onerous time-consuming demands which detract from the purpose of using them. At the heart of managing performance is the relationship between manager and member of staff i.e. the people part of the equation; tools are there to give structure, consistency and ensure alignment.

This section explores some of the common tools and explains why and how they are used.

Objectives

Objectives provide direction at all levels of organisations. They are statements of what needs to be achieved. You may be familiar with:

◆ Strategic objectives

◆ Corporate objectives

◆ Business objectives

◆ Marketing objectives

◆ Team objectives

◆ Individual or personal work objectives

◆ Development objectives.

They can cover a variety of timescales. For example, strategic objectives for an organisation could be for three to five years; individual or work objectives may be for the next month. Generally, the shorter term the objective the more precise it is.

Aims, goals and objectives

Aims or goals tend to be less specific and set direction rather than outcomes. Many organisations refer to strategic objectives when in fact they are phrased as more general aims or goals.

Objectives to manage performance

Everyone should know what the organisation needs them to achieve. A list of tasks, often taken from a job description, just isn't enough. Although a job description gives an outline of what's expected, personal work objectives give clear direction on what has to be achieved and by when. For example:

Task	Personal work objectives
A fundraiser knows he has to raise income	How much and by when
A HR manager knows he has to manage how performance is rewarded	When a new system has to have been researched, selected and implemented and within what constraints
A software development programmer knows he has to develop software	Exactly which project/part of a project has to be taken to what stage by when
A check-out assistant knows he has to serve customers	Dealing with difficult customers

Objectives generally fall into two main categories:

◆ Objectives that bring value, e.g. improving the way things are done, bringing in new processes or procedures, improving the quality of service offered to customers, reducing costs

◆ Objectives around essential outputs of the role, e.g. income targets.

 Key point

Personal work objectives provide a basis for managing performance and give focus to the individual.

Making objectives SMART

Objectives should meet the SMART criteria. SMART stands for:

S – Specific

M – Measurable

A – Agreed and Achievable

R – Realistic and Relevant

T – Timebound

> Get into the habit of checking that objectives meet the SMART criteria.

Specific

Specific refers to an objective having a clear outcome. It's easy when referring to quantitative measures. For example:

◆ Increase sales by 5%

◆ Recruit five support staff for new project

◆ Increase to 50 the number of orders processed in an hour.

But even when there is no quantitative measure, a specific outcome should be identified. For example:

◆ Research options for moving to a new site

◆ Deal with difficult customers with greater confidence

◆ Introduce a process for dealing with complaints.

Measurable

How will you know when the objective has been achieved? There has to be a 'finishing post' so it is clear when it has been reached. It might be expressed in quantitative terms or it may be a specific output, e.g. a report or a particular outcome, e.g. to an agreed set standard.

Sometimes it makes sense to have a series of measures or targets to monitor progress towards achieving an objective.

A software design team had an objective to get a new product on the market by the spring. Targets were set for each month to ensure delivery by the end of March.

A community fundraiser had an objective to pilot a charity auction in September. Targets in the run up to the auction included:

❖ sign-up endorsement of celebrity by May

❖ 100 promises by June, 200 by the end of July

❖ media coverage in local newspapers and local radio during August.

Missing any of the targets would give early warning that remedial action would have to be taken to ensure the success of the event.

Agreed and achievable

There is a huge difference between being given an objective and agreeing an objective. It's about ownership. Of course there will be circumstances when objectives are set. For example, if a team of five has a sales target of £1 million, each may have a target of £200,000. But there should also be scope for agreeing individual objectives, e.g. each member may have a different personal work objective such as:

◆ Grow market X by 10%

◆ Coach new member of team so she is ready to take over Y area.

Achievable refers to ability of the person. Do they have the necessary skills, knowledge and resources? If there's a skills gap it needs to closed – otherwise the objective is unlikely to be met.

Realistic and relevant

Realistic is straightforward. From past experience, is it realistic to expect someone to achieve the objective? Are there factors outside their control which will prevent it being met. A lack of resources is one of the most common reasons for failure to meet objectives.

Being relevant is about being relevant to the organisation. Objectives must contribute to the overall strategic objectives of the organisation.

Aligning to the strategic objectives

Strategic objective:
A local authority had a strategic objective to reduce their carbon footprint.

Alignment means:
An HR officer had an objective to implement the requirements of a government scheme to encourage the use of bicycles within six months.

Strategic objective:
A small charity, employing 40 people, had a strategic objective to increase money spent on the cause.

Alignment means:
The fundraising team was enlarged and their targets raised. However the administrative team leader had an objective to reduce spending on stationery supplies and re-negotiate contracts with local caterers to achieve cost reduction of 5% in his budget area.

Timebound

Objectives need a date by which they will be achieved. If it's a relatively short period of time it signals the need for a review to coincide with the target date for completion of the objective. If it's an objective which will span a year, then it's likely that there will be interim targets or stages which can be reviewed.

Activity

Decide whether the following objectives are Specific, Measurable and Timebound.

- ❖ Open retail outlet in Purbeck by end of current financial year
- ❖ Review and make recommendations for new HR system for discussion at next senior management team meeting
- ❖ Achieve 90% satisfaction rating in next quarter
- ❖ Achieve Investor in People status by end of year.

There is nothing so useless as doing efficiently that which should not be done at all.'

Peter Drucker

Although you have no knowledge of the context in which they are set, they do seem to be:

◆ Specific – it's clear what has to be achieved.

◆ Measurable – there will be a definite point at which you can judge whether or not they have been achieved.

◆ Timebound – there is a clear end-date for the objective to be achieved.

There is no way to judge their relevance or whether they are achievable within the constraints of the organisation and people.

Activity

Review your own work objectives. Do they meet the SMART criteria?

Review the objectives you set with your team. Are they SMART?

There are a host of reasons why people justify un-SMART objectives or the complete absence of objectives.

◆ 'We just don't know what we want the outcome to be.'

◆ 'They know what they've got to do – it's just a matter of getting on and doing it.'

◆ 'We sort of firm up on objectives as we go along.'

Don't be fooled. Failing to set objectives is an opportunity missed for two main reasons:

1 Objectives, set and used effectively, can have a big impact on motivation. (See *Expectancy theory* in Chapter 2.)

2 Lots of effort and resources can be spent producing outcomes which don't contribute to getting the organisation where it wants to go.

Tip

Make sure you know how you and your team contribute to your organisation – otherwise effective objective setting is difficult.

Measures, targets and KPIs

There's no denying it. If people are to be held accountable for their work then:

1 Some form of measures, targets or key performance indicators (KPIs) have to be set.

2 At some time, progress against the measures must be reviewed.

KPIs

KPIs are measures which help to monitor progress towards an objective or goal. They define key outcomes which need to be met if the overall objective is to be achieved. Some organisations call them measures or targets.

In some jobs, people are driven by measures. For example:

◆ Sales targets   ◆ Income targets

◆ Calls answered   ◆ Length of calls

◆ Problems solved in set times

◆ Accuracy rates.

Others introduce measures to ensure progress can be properly monitored. But there are potential pitfalls – measures can be irrelevant and demotivating.

What gets measured gets done.

Tom Peters

Making the measures relevant

Measures tend to be quantitative. That's no problem as long as they are measuring what's important.

Setting irrelevant measures is an easy trap to fall into. The culture of many organisations is to focus on quantitative measures – any measure is better than no measure at all. The problem can then be magnified if over-zealous effort and resources are put into ensuring pointless measures are then met.

Three rings

An insurance broking firm set a key performance indicator of answering 90% of calls within three rings. Staff were awarded a bonus on achievement of the KPI. However it was the satisfaction level of customers at the end of a call which had a direct impact on the business performance. The KPI meant that staff were focussed on achieving the 'three ring' KPI to the detriment of putting the effort into meeting customer expectations and, in turn, getting new business.

The debates in the media about performance of public services and the NHS often revolve about whether or not a particular target has been achieved and the relevance of the target in the first place. The same debate can be applied to many measures set in the workplace.

Measures and motivation

Performance measures are meant to motivate. To recap from Chapter 2, expectancy theory of motivation explains how the setting of measures provide first-level outcomes. These provide the stepping stones to second-level outcomes which are the valued reward.

But just as measures can be motivating, they can also be very demotivating if ill-conceived.

Groundless measures

Sarah was a newly appointed internal communications manager for a national retail company. One of her first tasks was to carry out a staff survey. The return rate for the previous survey, four years ago, has been 60%. Her line manager told Sarah that she wanted a return of over 80% and it was written into her first set of work objectives. Sarah spent an anxious three weeks monitoring return rates. The actual rate was 65% despite a competently developed and implemented communications plan. At the next work review Sarah's manager dismissed the 80% target saying that it was hardly surprising in the current wave of restructuring and redundancies. Sarah was left wondering the point was of having objectives.

> To make sure measures are relevant, ask yourself what will happen if they are met, and if they are not met. Then judge if they are relevant.

Balancing the measures

Try not to get focused on a very narrow set of measures, such as an income target or the number of customers processed.

Benefits of balancing

A small civil engineering company had a manic summer with the team focused on meeting the customer demand for feasibility studies and projects. Income targets were exceeded but by late September everything had gone quiet. The team realised that they had not had the time to do any marketing work over the summer and consequently as the summer projects neared completion there was nothing to replace them. A period of intense marketing activity followed which included tendering for new jobs, raising their profile in trade magazines and following up 'dormant' enquiries. By January monthly income was back on target. The team recognised they would have to maintain an appropriate level of marketing activity through busy periods if they were to reach their financial targets and set performance measures in relation to number of new contacts made and proposals submitted.

The lesson is simple and obvious. Potential early warning signs of problems ahead need to be spotted so that action can be taken *before* they make an impact on objectives. It's about balancing the measures so that they provide information which is going to be useful.

The balanced scorecard

In the 1990s Dr Robert Kaplan and Dr David Norton recognised that there was an over-reliance on financial indicators to measure the health of an organisation. They likened this approach to a pilot of a plane who only looked at one dial to establish if the plane was on course and functioning. They argued that organisations should plan, monitor and measure performance on a more balanced set of indicators – hence the term 'balanced scorecard'.

The suggested indicators should be identified in four main areas:

◆ Financial perspective

◆ Customer perspective

◆ Internal perspective (e.g. are the right processes in place?)

◆ Innovation and learning (e.g. how can we develop ourselves to continually create value?)

Activity

Using the case study of the civil engineering company above, in terms of Kaplan and Norton's balanced scorecard:

❖ What was the team failing to do initially?

❖ What steps did it take to remedy the situation?

Over the summer the team had been focusing on getting the jobs done to reach their financial targets. By introducing targets around marketing activity they were taking a more balanced approach. If they didn't achieve their marketing targets it would signal that there could be a potential lull in business ahead. Therefore a rapid re-focusing of marketing activity would be needed.

Monitor line management

Many organisations introduce measures around staff satisfaction with management of performance as a key indicator. As studies show that the greatest influence on motivation is the line manager, it makes sense to monitor perceptions of line management. Decreasing satisfaction in areas of the organisation can provide early warning of potential high staff turnover or decreased productivity.

Relection

Do you have measures?/Do you set them for members of your team?

Are they relevant?

Do they help or hinder your motivation?

Are they balanced?

Values

To recap from Chapter 1, many organisations have a set of values which aim to guide the behaviour of employees from the chief executive to front-line staff.

Why have values?

Values are designed to align behaviour. They can be used in a variety of ways. For example:

◆ To guide behaviour by providing a reference point for what is and what is not acceptable behaviour

◆ As a basis for a competency framework. For example, the exact behaviours around a specific value can be identified and used to review performance against.

> **Value: Integrity**
>
> In practice:
>
> ● Admitting mistakes – and learning from them
>
> ● Being honest with the facts
>
> ● Delivering on promises

◆ As a framework to help make decisions. For example, having a value around being environmentally responsible would help to make decisions about which suppliers to use or product specifications.

By encouraging employees to live the values, an organisation is able to align behaviour and influence the culture, i.e. the way things are done.

Living the values

Getting people to 'live the values' is where the challenge really lies.

Values have to be translated into specific examples of behaviour – otherwise they are worthless.

An area manager for a national housing association manages ten wardens. Each warden has responsibility for managing a residential home for older people. One of the values of the organisation is 'respect'. At a team meeting the wardens discussed what the word 'respect' meant in practice for them and came up with the following:

Caring for residents in a way you would want to be cared for (e.g. respect privacy)

Letting everyone have their say/opinions

Recognise people may need a little more 'input' or help to do something or understand something (be patient)

Makes sure what happens in the team stays in the team

RESPECT

Listen – really listen – before jumping to a judgement

If people are a bit off-colour or down – give them extra leeway

Give feedback constructively – negative and positive

To embed the value the manager asked each warden to identify for the next review meeting two occasions which showed how they had demonstrated respect.

Integrating values into objectives

Demonstration of values can directly be translated into performance management objectives. For example, line managers may have an objective around 'leading by example to demonstrate the values' for which they would collect evidence of what specific actions they have taken.

Creating team values

Values can provide a valuable tool in shaping team culture. If your organisation doesn't have values, then it leaves the potential for your team to develop its own.

For example, in a team meeting:

◆ Ask each member to identify up to six values which they feel are important to the way they should work as a team. Write each value on a separate piece of paper.

◆ Group the values into ones which are the same or very similar.

◆ Reach a consensus, for example by voting, on those values which will be adopted by the team.

◆ Identify behaviours which show the values in practice.

Values and corporate social responsibility

Corporate social responsibility (CSR) is a concept which has steadily been gaining momentum worldwide.

The Government sees CSR as the business contribution to our sustainable development goals. Essentially it is about how business takes account of its economic, social and environmental impacts in the way it operates – maximising the benefits and minimising the downsides.

www.csr.gov.uk (February 2007)

CSR Europe is a non-profit organisation that promotes corporate social responsibility. Our mission is to help companies achieve profitability, sustainable growth and human progress by placing corporate social responsibility in the mainstream of business practice.

www.csreurope.org (February 2007)

Putting values at the heart of organisations is one way in which corporate social responsibility is being developed.

Integrity

An IT consultancy had 'integrity' as one of its values. When a manager was asked how he translated the value into his working practices, his answer included:

❖ By not promising what we can't deliver.

❖ By revealing true costs and the reasoning behind them.

❖ By recognising confidentiality as an absolute.

❖ Openness and honesty in all transactions, e.g. if there's a problem we'll work it through with the client.

Checklist for embedding/developing values

- ☐ Provide clear guidance and training to make the links between the values and specific examples of behaviour
- ☐ Discuss the values with your team
- ☐ Encourage team members to identify values in each other's actions
- ☐ Celebrate demonstration of the values
- ☐ If your organisation hasn't got values, then develop values with your team.

Competency frameworks

Competency frameworks identify the skill, knowledge and behaviours needed for a particular role. The concept of competencies began to take hold in the early 1990s with the development of vocational qualifications. They now play a major role in recruitment and performance management for many organisations.

Types of competency frameworks

There are two main types:

◆ Frameworks which focus on describing outcomes of effective performance

◆ Behavioural frameworks which define the behaviours which lie behind achieving the outcomes of competent performance.

The two types of competency frameworks are shown in the national management and leadership standards. They describe both the outcomes of effective performance and the behaviours which underpin effective performance for the different levels of management. For example, the following competencies are taken from the National Occupational Standards for management and leadership:

A1: Manage own resources

Outcomes of effective performance

You must be able to do the following:

1 Identify and agree the requirements of your work role with those you report to.

2 Discuss and agree personal work objectives with those you report to and how you will measure progress.

3 Identify any gaps between the requirements of your work role and your current knowledge, understanding and skills.

4 Discuss and agree, with those you report to, a development plan to address any identified gaps in your current knowledge, understanding and skills.

....

Behaviours which underpin effective performance

1   You recognise changes in circumstances promptly and adjust plans and activities accordingly.

2   You prioritise objectives and plan work to make best use of time and resources.

3   You take responsibility for making things happen.

4   You take pride in delivering high quality work.

....

Source: www.management-standards.com

Many organisations develop their own competency frameworks which include a mixture of behaviours and outcomes which need to be developed and embedded throughout the organisation.

For example:

Competency: Relationship building

1   Shows sensitivity and understands others' perspectives.

2   Listens and takes account of stakeholder views – managing stakeholder needs effectively.

3   Demonstrates empathy and emotional intelligence.

4   Cultivates and maintains extensive informal networks.

5   Seeks out and builds mutually beneficial relationships.

6   Builds rapport, keeping others in the loop – for example, sharing plans, information and consulting widely.

7   Identifies and nurtures opportunities for collaboration & partnership working.

8   Handles difficult people and tense situations with diplomacy and tact.

9   Spots potential conflict, brings disagreements into the open, and helps de-escalate.

10 Encourages debate and open discussion and orchestrates win-win situations.

These tailored competency frameworks can then be used as a focus for recruitment and performance management.

| Competencies tested during recruitment and selection | → | Tailored competency framework | ← | Competencies used during performance management |

Competencies or competences?

Should you use the spelling competencies or competences? Some purists will argue there's a difference but in reality the spellings are interchangeable. Competencies is probably more widely used and can refer to both behaviours and outcomes.

Competencies in performance management

Competencies can be used to manage performance in two main ways.

1 For assessment

2 As a development tool.

Using competencies as an assessment tool

This applies more often when a job involves technical competencies which describe outcomes of effective performance.

Outcome-based assessment

Trainees at an oil refinery have to undergo a period of training. This involves an initial two-week classroom-based period followed by training 'on-the-job' under the direction of a 'coach'. At the end of the training period the trainee has to demonstrate competent performance against a set of competencies assessed by a plant manager.

There are competencies for each role at the refinery and promotion is dependent on assessment against the relevant competencies.

Clear standards of performance are essential for managing performance. They reduce ambiguity as to what is and is not expected. Although your organisation may not use a formal competency framework, the principle of agreeing what constitutes the required level of performance is fundamental to:

◆ Managing performance (Chapter 4).

◆ Taking action resulting from under-performance (Chapter 6).

Using competencies as a development tool

For this use, these are normally competency frameworks which define a mixture of outcomes and behaviours. They provide an invaluable tool to set the agenda for discussing performance.

Developing skills and behaviours

A telecom company developed competency frameworks for senior, middle and operational managers. During a work review a service manager and his line manager agreed that the competency 'Empowering people to take decisions and operate on their own initiative' was essential behaviour in his job role. They agreed that neither of them could think of examples of the manager proactively empowering his team. By reviewing the criteria of the empowerment competency they set the following objective:

◆ Create a forum for the team to discuss and find solutions to operational difficulties by January 31.

Tip

If you have a competency framework, then use it. Few are perfect and there is bound to be wording with which you disagree. However, overall, they provide a sound framework for discussion – don't get too hung up on the detail.

360-degree feedback

360-degree feedback, sometimes referred to as multi-source feedback, is a process which captures perceptions of a person's performance from a range of people. This can include direct reports, colleagues, stakeholders in other organisations and/or customers. This feedback is combined with line manager observations and self-review.

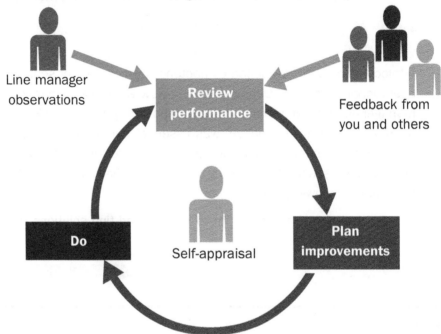

Figure 3.1 360-degree feedback and performance management

It can identify strengths and weaknesses which would otherwise be missed by a line manager and individual. In other words it can build a much more holistic, and accurate, picture of performance.

Key point

The aim of 360-degree feedback is to give a more rounded picture of a person's performance and the impact they have on others.

How is feedback collected?

Usually a form is sent out or e-mailed. The content depends on which competencies are important to the organisation. For example, it might be a series of statements against which the person giving feedback is asked for a reaction or it may take the respondent down the route of thinking of specific behavioural examples.

Attributes	Response	☑	Examples
Promotes a no-blame culture	Agree strongly Agree Disagree Disagree strongly	☐ ☐ ☐ ☐	
Seeks out and acknowledges those who make a difference	Agree strongly Agree Disagree Disagree strongly	☐ ☐ ☐ ☐	

Competency: Provides effective leadership

1 Please tick the appropriate box if you can think of specific examples when the person showed the behaviour.

☐ Articulates a vision that generates excitement and enthusiasm

☐ Articulates a vision that generates commitment

☐ Creates a sense of common purpose

☐ Encourages and supports others to take decisions

☐ Inspires others, championing work to achieve common goals

☐ Balances agendas and builds consensus

☐ Allows others to wander off-track without attempting to refocus them

☐ Does not attempt to sell the vision for the organisation

☐ Does not identify barriers to achieving common goals or work to overcome these

☐ Unrealistically enthusiastic about what can be achieved

☐ Appears unenthusiastic and hesitant

☐ Persists with unsuccessful approaches

Source: www.nfp-resourcing.co.uk

How it works in practice

The feedback may be given anonymously to external consultants, HR departments or line managers. This means that there have to be enough people involved to ensure anonymity. The people giving the feedback, i.e. the 'raters', should be fully briefed – which includes understanding what will happen to the responses they give.

Alternatively feedback can be given openly. This tends to work in more mature organisations which already have a culture of openness and transparency.

Choice as to who is asked to give feedback usually depends on the purpose of the 360-degree process.

Using 360 for development

This is the most common use for 360-degree feedback. Development objectives and plans are formed as a result of the combined feedback.

The impact and usefulness of 360-degree feedback usually declines over time. When used regularly the quality of the feedback tends to reduce as people get bored or feel little has changed since last time.

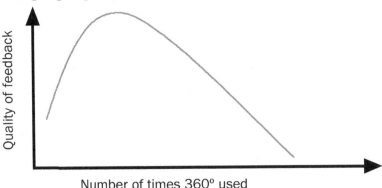

Using 360 to appraise performance

360-degree feedback can be linked directly to reward, e.g. performance related pay and promotions. Care has to be taken over its introduction and a potential pitfall is that feedback is less honest. It is also impossible to guarantee that all feedback is accurate and objective and therefore care must be taken that the feedback is treated only as one source of evidence for appraisal purposes.

Informal 360

Getting into the habit of asking for feedback from people you work with is good practice. It can be customers, your peers, team members, anyone who observes you at work.

Why bother?

To develop you need to learn. Learning involves reflecting on some form of input. Chapter 2 looked at the opportunities reflecting on our own behaviour gives. Equally important is the ability to reflect on the feedback that we pick up from other people.

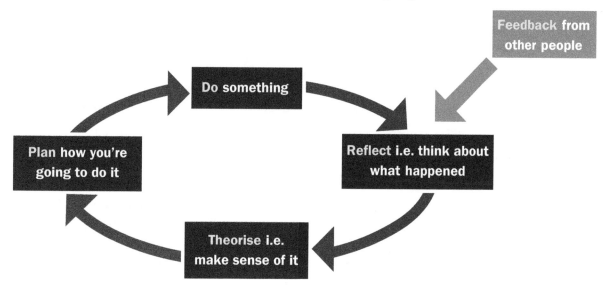

How to get informal feedback

Probably the simplest way is to just ask. However, it's helpful if you think through specifically what you want feedback on beforehand. Taking someone by surprise and asking what they think of some aspect of your performance is not likely to result in quality feedback.

As a project to develop new procedures drew to a close, Ralph ask the project team to rate him on his performance in three key areas:

1 Communication

2 Responding to pressure

3 Leadership.

He explained that he was keen to develop and learn from the project and would appreciate pointers as to how he could improve. They agreed and he made sure he met each of the team informally for 5–10 minutes to receive their feedback.

Whatever you do:

◆ Keep things simple – ask for feedback on a few key areas. People will be more inclined to spend the time than if you make the process over-complex.

◆ Be ready to use the feedback.

Activity

How can you get feedback on your performance from the people you work with?

What mechanisms could you encourage your team to use to build a more holistic picture of their performance?

Managers who most effectively manage the performance of their teams are also good at communicating. Be willing to talk, discuss, ask questions. Anything that increases your understanding of your team and encourages communication will enhance your success at managing performance.

 For more on constructive feedback see Chapter 4, for more on communications skills see Chapter 5.

One-to-one meetings

Meetings to manage performance come in all shapes and sizes. At one end of the spectrum is the annual meeting which formally reviews performance over the past year, followed by objective setting for the forthcoming year. This type of meeting is often referred to as the 'annual appraisal meeting' or 'performance review'. It's usually documented and kept on file.

At the other extreme it could be a short, 5-10 minute meeting, to update on recent progress on a particular project and deal with any issues.

Whatever their scale, one-to-one meetings are an essential tool in the performance management process.

'Put Monty back on his branch, you were due in my office half an hour ago for your performance review.'

How frequent should meetings be?

Although there are likely to be only one or two formal meetings which are synchronised with the organisation's planning cycle; work reviews to discuss performance should take place regularly.

Horses for courses

We have our annual appraisal in June. That's because the new business plan is finalised in March. It's a major meeting. To prepare, I complete documentation which asks me things about what went well, or not, in the year. My line manager does the same. Every six weeks we meet to have a one-to-one. They're a bit like mini-appraisals but we tend to focus on successes and problem areas rather than everything.

I rarely see my line manager and when I do it's a frenzy of activity bringing each other up-to-date. However once a year we do meet to formally review my performance against some corporate standards of performance. If there's a problem we talk on the phone. I'm pretty much left to my own devices. It seems to work.

Everyone's experience of performance management is likely to be different. But examples of 'best practice' look like this.

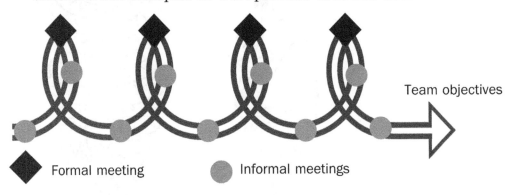

Team objectives

◆ Formal meeting   ● Informal meetings

Figure 3.2   Performance management cycles in practice

It's about making sure time is dedicated to discussing performance at regular intervals. This may be face-to-face or it could be by phone. How often and for how long will depend on your circumstances.

Q. How often should meetings be?

A. As often as is needed for both sides to feel that performance is being managed effectively.

What should happen in a meeting?

Any meeting could potentially include:

◆ Reviewing performance

◆ Evaluation of any development activity

◆ Setting objectives and/or performance measures

◆ Identifying development needs.

Or in the case of a short regular meeting, it might simply be a quick review of how things are going against performance measures.

What's essential is that time is given, regularly, to discussing performance. That's what managing performance is all about. There are no shortcuts and any effective process demands a time commitment.

The documentation

Most organisations supply documentation to record the outcomes of formal meetings. Sometimes there may be a part for the manager and team member to complete beforehand, which could include:

◆ Reviewing performance and actions resulting from previous meetings;

◆ Identifying potential training needs.

Documentation is usually signed by both parties and filed.

Checklist for designing documentation

☐ Identify the purpose(s) of the documentation.

☐ Pilot it before implementation – gather lots of feedback; check it works.

☐ Issue clear guidance explaining who should do what and when.

☐ Keep it simple.

☐ Introduce a document control system to ensure only current version is used.

Summary

◆ There are a number of common tools used to help manage performance such as SMART objectives, measures, KPIs, targets, values, competencies and one-to-one meetings.

◆ Take care. At the heart of managing performance are good working relation-ships. Tools give structure, consistency and ensure alignment. They should support rather than drive the process.

◆ Personal work objectives provide focus for the individual and align perform-ance across the organisation. They should be SMART.

◆ Measures, targets and KPIs ensure direction and accountability. They must be relevant, motivate performance and be balanced.

◆ Values aim to guide behaviour within an organisation. When living the values is a high priority, organisations often integrate a review of behaviour against the values into performance management.

◆ Competency frameworks define the behaviours and outcomes required of employees. Performance can be reviewed against them and development needs identified where appropriate.

◆ One-to-one meetings (face-to-face or phone) set the stage for managing performance. They must take place regularly.

4 The skills

The skills of managing performance

What do you need to do to manage performance? At one level the answer is to embed the performance management cycle within your team. But this requires skills which include:

- Assessing performance
- Giving constructive feedback
- Setting work objectives
- Identifying development needs
- Supporting development
- Managing one-to-one meetings.

The skills are the same for anyone who manages performance – from team leader level up to senior manager. Seniority doesn't demand more complex abilities. At any level, you simply need to put the skills into practice.

Tip

If your role is to achieve results through people, then managing their performance is a top priority. Spend time on it. Otherwise you won't achieve the results.

William monitored the clowns' performance daily – he was convinced the success of the show depended upon accuracy, and nothing to do with laughter...

Assessing performance

The failure to assess performance lies at the root of many performance management problems. If you can't, or don't, assess performance it means that it becomes very difficult, if not impossible, to:

◆ Know if objectives or targets have been met

◆ Give feedback on performance

◆ Keep records

◆ Identify development needs.

In a nutshell, if you don't assess performance, you can't manage it.

The essential ingredient

It's essential to have a benchmark against which to assess performance. It might be one or a combination of:

◆ Work objectives   ◆ Measures

◆ Competencies   ◆ Tasks in the job description.

There has to be something that describes the standard of performance you're expecting, or is expected of you. You then need to:

1 Collect 'evidence'.

2 Evaluate the evidence against the standard.

Sounds daunting, but in practice it doesn't have to take long and dramatically increases the quality of the feedback you can give.

Collecting the 'evidence'

Evidence = anything that contributes to showing whether the standard of performance has been met

This is about collecting examples of outcomes or behaviour. At its simplest level it may be a matter of finding out what progress has been made towards achieving an objective or target. For example:

◆ Have the sales or income target been achieved?

- ◆ Was the report completed?
- ◆ Were the targeted number of training courses delivered?
- ◆ Was the software system installed?

Specific outcomes are usually relatively straightforward to assess; behaviours can often be more difficult.

Activity

Consider the behaviours under the competency introduced in Chapter 3 on relationship building (page 51). Supposing you had to convince someone that you were skilled at relationship building. Pick one of the criteria. What examples would you give to show that you had demonstrated it?

Here's one manager's response.

I had two internal applicants for a post. There wasn't much between them and the one who performed the best during the selection process was chosen. I could see that there was potential for conflict because Nicola, who hadn't got the job, actually had more experience. The day the appointment was announced I arranged to meet with Nicola and gave her detailed feedback on what had come over in the interview, as her strengths and weaknesses. I felt that by the end of the meeting she was a lot more positive and was talking about developing her IT skills.

Has the manager convinced you of his ability to, 'spot potential conflict, brings disagreements into the open, and helps de-escalate'? You may want to ask a few questions but overall it's a good example and is on track for getting a tick in the box on an appraisal form.

Source of evidence

Your observations are likely to be a key component of the evidence you collect. What have you heard of seen which shows whether of not someone is performing as you would expect? Other sources of evidence could be peers, customers and self-review.

What's essential is that some form of benchmark is set so that the expectations of performance are clear. It's then a matter of collecting evidence so assessment can be made and feedback given.

Making notes

Keep a record of your observations on an on-going basis and any other inputs. For example:

> *7/11*
>
> *Observed Pat dealing with an angry client. Initially dealt with her well, staying calm, listening, making sure he got the full story. Then seemed at a loss to know where to direct her and started to get defensive and then irritated.*

If you don't make even the briefest notes of observations, feedback from other people or incidents it becomes very difficult to evaluate performance against the standard. It also means that any judgements you make about performance will be based on recent events – it's often hard to remember what happened two or three months ago; just about impossible to remember any longer.

Evaluating against the standards

This is the time to judge the degree to which the standards are being met and back up your judgement with some evidence. For example:

Judgement
→

Paul's doing really well. He's met all his targets and I've received positive feedback from two suppliers about his manner and how he's willing to go that extra mile for them.   ↑ Evidence

Judgement
→

Sabina is underperforming. The report she did for me last week needed rewriting, she's been late at least five times in the last three weeks and I've received a request to supply figures to finance that she should have done.'   ↑ Evidence

What's important is to have the examples on which to base your assessment. Otherwise you can't make an informed assessment of performance and you won't be able to give effective feedback.

 Avoid the 'halo' and 'horns' effect, i.e. if someone has performed well or poorly in one area you assume that's how they are performing in all areas. Systematic assessment of performance will prevent that happening.

Giving constructive feedback

Giving feedback is probably the most powerful skill to help motivate and prevent performance issues. It's also the one which is least effectively used, probably because:

1　You've first got to assess performance.

2　Preparing to give feedback requires time.

3　It's easy to avoid doing it, or doing it at a superficial level.

Preparing to give feedback

Before you can give constructive feedback you need to prepare. You need to:

Allocate some time to think

It you've assessed performance then it shouldn't take long. But you need to think through how to put the feedback across.

Consider the person on the receiving end

It's not just about communicating the feedback. It's about communicating it in a way that will then be used to help learn and develop. The best, and quickest, way is to talk about the feedback-giving process with the person beforehand:

◆　What's been their experience of receiving feedback?

◆　What sort of feedback have they found most useful?

◆　What sort of feedback has been least useful?

Just because you like feedback to be given in a certain way, doesn't necessarily mean that it works best like that for everyone.

Make feedback specific

Focus your feedback on behaviour and performance not attitude and personality - especially when it's feedback on poor performance.

✘　Your whole attitude is wrong. You're surly to customers and abrupt with other people...

✓ There have been three occasions when we've had complaints from customers. I overheard Graham asking you to help last week and you came across quite aggressively telling him it was not your responsibility.

But even when it's feedback on good performance, it should be specific.

✓ Your attention to detail is excellent. When I read your report I noticed that you had followed up references and done really thorough research.

Plan the order for giving feedback

Where possible give positive feedback first and last. It is generally best to start and end on a positive note. Of course, the part in between has to be constructive; focusing on behaviours and performance rather than personality and attitudes!

'Ah, Waiter, soup; wonderful, a super start to the meal – main course; not so keen, a little underdone, and what was the mushy green veg? Pudding; jam roly-poly washed down with a nice Chianti – what can I say? A delightful finish, first class, my compliments to the chef.'

Giving the feedback

Feedback should be given regularly or as soon as possible after a particular event or incident. It doesn't have to take long. Five or ten minutes is often all that is necessary. But always make sure that you:

◆ Allocate enough time – giving feedback well sends strong messages that a person is valued; otherwise why would you bother spending your time on them?

◆ Choose somewhere private.

◆ Make sure you're not interrupted.

◆ Suggest ways forward; if behaviour has to change, then what alternative routes could be taken?

◆ Create a dialogue. Give the person an opportunity to ask questions and engage in discussion.

Before/during/after

Make notes. Keep a record of what feedback was given, especially when it's feedback on poor performance.

Take note

If the situation deteriorates and you need to go down the path of disciplinary action, you must have a record of your discussions around performance. This may sound negative, but is worth being aware of. There are legal implications if the actions result in dismissal and you must be able to show that you have done everything properly, all the way down the line.

Setting work objectives

Objectives:

◆ Must align with the team/department/organisation. Otherwise they have little or no value and resources are wasted.

◆ Should meet the SMART criteria.

Chapter 1 explores the importance of alignment and Chapter 3 looks at using objectives as an effective performance management tool.

So how skilled are you at setting objectives? Do they provide focus and direction? Would you miss them if they weren't set?

How valuable are your work objectives?

One of the key ingredients of high performance is giving people the opportunity to contribute – people perform better when they are actively invited to contribute to decisions, e.g. about their job, the environment, the way things work in the organisation. They also need to feel that their skills and knowledge are valued and used. Discussing the value of the objective-setting process you use and how it can be improved provides an opportunity for people to contribute.

Activity

Below are some questions. Ask people in your team to answer them and discuss their feedback with a view to improving the objective-setting process. Answer them yourself and you may find it can start a useful discussion with your line manager.

1 If you did not have work objectives, would you miss them?

☐ Yes ☐ No ☐ Partly

2 Do you understand how your work objectives contribute to the wider objectives of your team/department?

☐ Yes ☐ No ☐ Partly

3 Do you understand how your work objectives contribute to what your organisation is trying to achieve?

☐ Yes ☐ No ☐ Partly

4 Do you find your work objectives help you focus on your priorities?

☐ Yes ☐ No ☐ Partly

5 Are your work objectives realistic?

☐ Yes ☐ No ☐ Partly

6 Do you find that your work objectives help to increase/sustain your motivation?

☐ Yes ☐ No ☐ Partly

You may need to tailor the wording but the principle of discussing the setting of work objectives is sound. In so many organisations setting objectives degenerates into a pointless paper exercise and the opportunity to manage performance more effectively is lost.

Prioritising objectives

There are times when objectives need to be prioritised. Few people, if any, have the luxury of being able to focus on one objective at a time. Rather than leaving a member of your team to work out priorities, it can be useful if this becomes part of any objective-setting exercise. It can also act as a check to confirm that the objectives set are realistic.

Urgency and importance

George is publishing manager for a company which develops training materials. At director level the decision was taken to buy-in the rights to a new series of materials and re-design them to reflect the corporate brand, ready to launch in September. George knew he couldn't absorb the work and meet his other objectives. After a review with his line manager when they looked at the projected income for different products, the rebranding of the new materials became a priority as this was a key feature of achieving the strategic objective of entering new markets. His objective relating to updating an existing series was put on hold until the following spring.

Common reasons why people find work objectives unrealistic:

◆ Unachievable targets

◆ Unrealistic timescales

- ◆ Lack of budget/resources
- ◆ Too many conflicting demands on time
- ◆ Lack of support from line manager
- ◆ Lack of support from team
- ◆ Lack of support from other areas of the organisation.

Tip

Be stretching, be challenging but also be realistic. When failing to meet objectives becomes the norm it has a demotivating effect on all involved.

Setting objectives for repetitive jobs

Some jobs consist of a series of fairly repetitive tasks. It can seem difficult to set objectives which don't simply repeat the main responsibilties of the job. If you find this:

1 Acknowledge the problem.

2 Ask your team members – are there any areas they feel they could develop and add value to the team? Are there are any areas for personal development?

Involving your team and actively searching for areas to develop can be motivating for everyone as well as bringing beneficial outputs for the team.

Reviewing objectives

A year is a long time. Setting objectives and filing them away until the next annual review is a pointless exercise. Therefore make sure objectives are kept under review and broken down into smaller milestones if appropriate. They don't have to be reviewed in every one-to-one but they should be seen as a tool for focusing work priorities.

> Make objective-setting a valuable exercise. If you suspect it's not, then challenge what's happening.

Identifying development needs

Developing people is a key part of performance management. From an organisational perspective you need staff with skills and knowledge to meet the business need. If there's a gap, it has to be filled.

But development shouldn't always be the result of a skills gap. Creating an environment in which development is encouraged and valued brings a whole range of benefits for both the individual and the organisation.

The personal benefits of development

Personal development can help you feel good about yourself. For example, it can:

1   Satisfy a need to develop your potential. Some people just like to learn. In Maslow's terms it's about the need for personal fulfilment, right at the top of the hierarchy.

2   Be enjoyable.

3   Show that you're valued if your employer spends resources on you or if your manager makes time to help you to develop.

4   Provide the way to taking on more interesting, varied or challenging work.

5   Provide the means for promotion or moving to a better job.

Activity

People who have opportunities to develop new skills at work tend to be more motivated than those who don't.

Which of the reasons listed above is likely to impact most on increasing motivation to perform?

Being shown that you are valued by your manager and organisation is likely to have the most direct impact on level of motivation to perform.

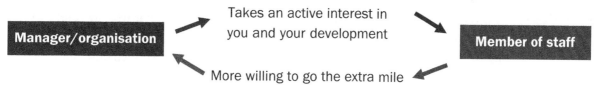

Manager/organisation → Takes an active interest in you and your development → Member of staff

More willing to go the extra mile

Identifying development needs

Development needs are commonly identified at the point of selection.

Many organisations have induction courses which can include a range of compulsory training programmes so a common standard is reached, e.g. health and safety or equal opportunities training. There may also be job-specific development needs for a particular role.

> When you recruit, spend time checking for any skills gaps. It's often easier to plan how to close the gap before the person becomes immersed in the role.

Then there are emerging development needs which result from reviews of performance or the setting of new work objectives.

Developing to meet new challenges

A service manager in a disability charity saw the potential demand for training in other organisations around the implications of the Disability Discrimination Act (DDA) for businesses. Research in the local area showed that it provided potential for an additional income stream for the charity. The advocacy officer, who had a training background, was eager to take on the objective of raising £10,000 through delivering training in the next financial year by using a network of consultant trainers. However, alongside the work objective she agreed two development objectives to prepare her to take on the new dimension to her role:

- Develop knowledge of the DDA by end of April
- Refresh training skills by end of April.

Research showed that 95% of organisations see the identification of training needs as one of the main purposes of a performance management system.

Managing Performance, No 86, April 2001, The Industrial Society

> ## The difference between training and development
>
> The terms are often used interchangeably. However, training usually refers to specific skills being delivered through some form of programme; development is about what's happening to the individual. i.e. the individual develops, often by undergoing training.

Meeting development needs

The main methods include:

- Attending training courses
- Coaching
- Shadowing
- Delegation
- Self-study (print-based or online) with tutor or line manager support.

Sometimes there is one obvious route. For example, if an organisation has developed its own in-house training then it would make sense to use it. However, if there are alternatives then responsibility for selecting can be delegated to your team member.

Meeting the need

'If we identify a development need in a one–to-one, we set the development objectives and then I leave it to my member of staff to source the best way he or she feels the objectives can be met. They've used just about every method you could think of; from enrolling on an Open University distance course to being coached by a colleague.'

Personal development planning

Staff who have a personal development plan, and who have received a formal performance appraisal within the past year, have significantly higher engagement levels than those who have not.

IES report 408, April 2004

Personal development planning can include the whole spectrum from identifying and meeting specific skills gaps to developing for the future benefit of the individual and the organisation.

What's important is that the development is captured on a plan which is used as a working document throughout the year. For example:

Personal Development Plan: Frank Miles					Plan updated: 3/9	
Task	Month					
	July	August	Sept	Oct	Nov	Dec
Presentation skills						
Source external presentation skills courses & agree with Ken	**Agreed to go to Vista training**					
Attend presentation skills course		**21-22 Aug**				
Deliver internal presentation on ISO 9000			18 Sept at Crawley site			
Review presentation – one-to-one meet			20 Sept			
Experience of chairing meetings						
Shadow Ken in SMT meetings			21-Sep	08-Oct		
Read up theory			By end Sept			
Meet with Saheed, 'guru' of chairing				3 or 4/10		
Plan to chair ISO meeting with Ken				By end of month		
Chair ISO meeting					05-Nov	
Feedback session with Ken					06-Nov	

✓ Elevating personal development plans to the status of working documents demonstrates that development is being taken seriously in your team.

✗ Jotting down a few actions at the end of appraisal documentation which is then filed until the following annual review equates to indulging in pointless bureaucracy.

Not every need is a development need

It's tempting to think of any under-performance in terms of being a development need. Don't make the mistake of jumping to that conclusion. It could be:

◆ Poor communication around expectations.

- ◆ Lack of motivation to perform. Here, encouraging development opportunities and showing an interest may enhance motivation and, in turn, performance. Just don't assume it's a skills gap.

- ◆ Lack of empowerment (i.e. being given the resources and authority to perform). Here delegation may be a way forward.

Training courses don't always close skills gaps

Activity

Consider the last four or five training courses you have attended. Estimate roughly the percentage of knowledge and skills you have transferred into the workplace from each one.

Unless people are highly motivated to develop themselves, transfer to the workplace tends to be low for a variety of reasons including:

- ◆ The objectives of the training course are unclear or inappropriate.

- ◆ There is no support for the transfer of learning from managers.

- ◆ The application of new skills and knowledge is not rewarded.

- ◆ Other colleagues lack new skills so momentum for implementation is lost.

- ◆ Opportunities to apply new skills are denied.

Research has shown that up to 87% of knowledge and skills covered in off-the-job training is lost within three months. However when structured, planned workplace coaching is used, transfer of learning is greatly improved (around 90% of skills and knowlege being retained).

Take note

Sending people on training courses can be highly effective as long as you support the transfer of skills into the workplace. As a manager you have a responsibility to do that.

Supporting development

Anyone who stops learning is old, whether at 28 or 80. Anyone who keeps learning stays young. The greatest thing in life is to keep your mind young.

Henry Ford

Development is about learning. To learn you go through the learning cycle. We're all expert at learning. From the day we are born we begin a steep learning curve. However, most people find that they learn more effectively when there is some form of support.

Supporting learning in practice

Supporting learning is an essential part of any line manager's role.

Activity

Consider the sample Personal Development Plan on page 77. If Ken is the line manager, what role is he playing in supporting Frank's development?

The Personal Development Plan seems to indicate that Ken is taking a very supportive role in Frank's development. He's empowering Frank to find a presentation skills course but wants to discuss Frank's findings. There's also an opportunity for Frank to review his performance after delivering his first presentation at a timely one-to-one. They've also agreed a very structured plan to support Frank through gaining the skills and knowledge to chair a meeting.

In total, between July and November, Ken is probably committing between two to three hours of his time to supporting Frank's development. Not a huge investment in terms of time but it is likely to have a range of benefits in terms of Frank's performance. Not only is Ken actively engaging in discussion and therefore helping the learning process; he also demonstrating that Frank is sufficiently valued to warrant time spent on him.

Transferring learning to the job

Where skills or knowledge have been gained outside the job it's tempting to assume that they'll be transferred. But most people need, or would appreciate, a bit of help.

A standard process could look like this.

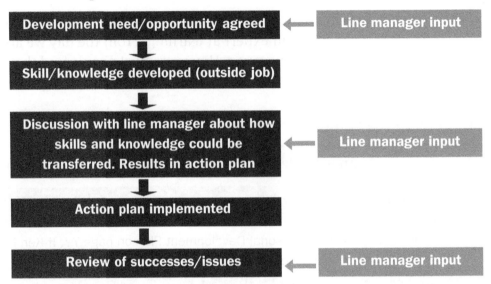

Following a process makes it easier to build the actions into a personal development plan; less chance of the learning being forgotten.

Learning in the role

The principle of supporting learning is the same when workplace activity is used as a vehicle for development, e.g. through delegation or coaching.

See *Coaching* in this series

A coach: 'sets mutually agreed targets with individuals and teams, plans how to achieve them, then delegates the authority to get on with it and monitors but doesn't intervene in the reality – the "eyes on and hands off" approach.'

Bob Garrett, *Creating a Learning Organisation*

Coaching involves a continuous cycle of planning, doing and then reviewing.

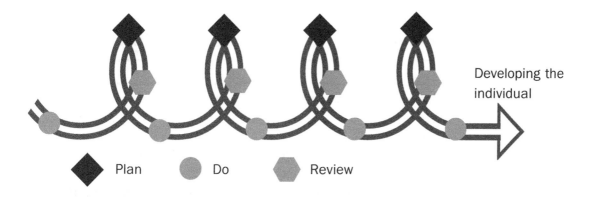

◆ Plan ● Do ⬡ Review

Activity

Use the following checklist to assess how well you support your team to develop.

Do you:

❖ Identify development needs?

❖ Have a process for recording development needs?

❖ Build in activities to ensure transfer to the workplace?

❖ Make sure all members of your team have a personal development plan?

Supporting development has to include spending time, individually, with your team members. It's got to be done on a regular basis rather than during a one-off annual review. But it doesn't have to be face-to-face and it doesn't have to take long.

Remote support

Although I'm sitting at my desk in Sheffield and my manager is in London we have monthly work reviews. He always checks on whether I'm adequately skilled for each contract and if there's any doubt we talk about how I could develop my skills. For example, I had to cost a project and it was new territory for me. Therefore we scheduled two thirty-minute phone calls when Martin would take me through examples of costings he'd done. In the meantime I'd dig out my old notes on costing to remind myself of what I knew about ten years ago.

It works well. I never feel that I'm going to be left struggling out of my depth.

Managing one-to-one meetings

Get to know the policies and procedures relating to performance management in your organisation. Ask the Human Resources department if you're in any doubt.

One-to-one meetings can range from a formal annual performance review or appraisal taking over an hour, to short informal discussions related to performance, planning and/or development. But the way they are managed will be similar.

1   Establish what do you want to achieve?

Managing an effective one-to-one meeting starts with being clear about:

◆   The purpose of the meeting;

◆   What you want to get out of the meeting;

◆   What the other person wants to get out of the meeting (you'll only find this out by asking – don't assume you know).

Activity

Select forthcoming one-to-one meetings. For each, identify the purpose (s), e.g. to:

☐   Review performance formally (over 6/12 months)

☐   Review progress against short-term targets

☐   Informal review of progress

☐   Opportunity to identify any issues

☐   Plan performance (over what time-span?)

☐   Plan development

☐   Identify development needs

☐   Transfer learning to the job

☐   Recognise achievements

☐   Address poor performance

☐   Other: ... ...

2 Prepare

This is about:

◆ Agreeing an agenda for the meeting so it achieves its purpose.

◆ Setting aside enough time – up to two hours for a formal review.

◆ Gathering the necessary information, observations and questions.

◆ Choosing the location – a motorway café can be perfectly adequate for an informal meeting but may not be ideal for an annual performance review.

◆ Making sure that you brief your team member so he/she can prepare. Your organisation may use a self appraisal form; or you can develop questions for them to consider before the meeting.

3 Manage the meeting

You've got your agenda and you both come to the meeting prepared. Then it's down to your communication skills. Aim to:

◆ Put the person at ease, e.g. ask how they see things, what have been their successes.

◆ Listen more than you speak – i.e. more than 50% of the time.

◆ Ask open questions which encourage reflection – it contributes to the learning process. They lead people to giving a more detailed response than a 'yes' or 'no' answer. They usually start with words such as, 'Why', How, 'What', or Where'.

I keep six honest serving-men
(They taught me all I knew);
Their names are What and Why and When
And How and Where and Who.

Rudyard Kipling

◆ Welcome and build on contributions and feedback.

Funnelling down

Don't expect one open question to always give a sufficiently detailed response. The *funnel technique* starts by answering a broad general question and then probes deeper with secondary questions.

What do you think have been the biggest challenges in the last quarter?

Why do you say that?

What was particular challenging about that one?

What would you have done differently, knowing what you do now?

Tip

Make sure the meeting isn't interrupted. Turn off your mobile phones. And do use comfortable chairs.

4 After the meeting

Follow up any actions, as soon as possible. If formal notes are needed you will both need to agree them – aim to write them up within the week

Take note

There should be no surprises in a formal review. Regular one-to-ones mean that you are both always up-to-date on what's happening.

Summary

◆ Managing performance needs you to be skilled at:

- ◆ Assessing performance

- ◆ Giving constructive feedback

- ◆ Setting work objectives

- ◆ Identifying development needs

- ◆ Supporting development

- ◆ Managing one-to-one meetings.

◆ Assess performance objectively before giving constructive feedback – being aware of the 'halo' and 'horns' effect.

◆ Giving feedback constructively is a powerful motivator. Always spend time thinking through how to give the feedback and give it regularly.

◆ Work objectives align the organisation as well as giving direction and a focus for priorities. Make sure they meet the SMART criteria.

◆ Identifying development needs and supporting development is an integral part of the performance management process. Allocate time to making sure that learning is transferred.

◆ One-to-one meetings provide the main vehicle for managing performance. Be clear about what you want to get out of each meeting. There should no surprises in a formal performance review or appraisal meeting.

 Do not cancel or cut short meetings. Managing your team to get results should be your No. 1 priority.

5 Creating the culture

Team culture

Managing performance = creating a culture in which people want to work to the best of their ability.

The culture of a team or organisation can best be described as, 'the way things are done around here'. It's that unwritten set of rules for operating. For example, who washes the cups, what happens if someone is under pressure, do senior managers get parking spaces closest to the door?

Every organisation will have its own dominant culture but so will each team or department.

Activity

Your behaviour will have a big influence on the culture of your team.

Try this quick assessment of the people you manage. Do they:

☐ Get a sense of achievement from the work they do?

☐ Volunteer to help out when things get pressured?

☐ Enjoy coming to work?

☐ Admit mistakes?

☐ Want to go that extra mile?

The culture you create will depend on you and your style of management. That's why it's so important to increase your awareness the 'human dimension' and the impact of your own behaviour.

This chapter focuses on some of the very practical ways that you can use to influence the culture of your working environment. They are based on the theories of motivation introduced in Chapter 2. Simple things, many of which you may already do, which create the right environment for managing performance.

Being a good communicator

Poor communication is the root of many problems. Either people don't bother communicating at all, assuming that someone else can read their mind, or the message sent isn't received as intended.

It's a problem that doesn't seem to be improving.

Two-thirds of American workers contacted said that poor communication prevents them from doing their best at work.

Poor Communications, *Newsweek*, 12th August 1996

In the Ashridge Management Index, reported 24th August 2006, poor communication topped the list of management challenges.

www.management-issues.com (February 2007)

What is effective communication?

Effective communication is a two-way process. It needs a sender and a receiver. It also needs feedback from the receiver to let the sender know the message has been received and understood.

Although the process is simple, there are many common pitfalls. It's probably impossible to eliminate all of the pitfalls; there are times when everyone is bound to make communication errors. However, being aware of the pitfalls can help to guard against them.

Common pitfalls

There are plenty of these and they include:

1   You choose the wrong words, e.g. they're confusing, too complicated, full of jargon.

2   You make false assumptions about the receiver's level of understanding.

3 The words may get distorted in the process of sending them, e.g. a noisy environment.

4 The receiver isn't listening.

5 The receiver doesn't understand.

6 The wrong channel is used, e.g. e-mail instead of a phone call.

Activity

Identify a couple of recent occasions when communication wasn't successful.

❖ What were the causes?

❖ What would have helped?

Any unsuccessful communication can be dissected to identify the root causes. It's useful to be able to identify them so you can learn for another time. However, taking a pragmatic approach, if you get into the habit of checking that your message has been received by getting some feedback, any problems can be put right immediately.

Get some feedback!

Getting feedback to confirm that the message has been understood is the most neglected part of the communication process. But if you don't get it, you have no way of knowing if you have communicated effectively. So, check!

Ask your team

The best way to learn and make improvements is to get some feedback from your team on your skills as a 'sender' in the communication process. For example, do you:

◆ Keep them informed about matters which affect their job?

◆ Keep them informed about matters which affect them?

◆ Choose the best channel to give information? Have there been any instances when a different channel would have been more appropriate?

◆ Communicate at the right time?

- Give the right level of detail/too much/too little?

- Have a habit of making assumptions about their level of knowledge?

- Ever seem patronising?

Activity

Introduce communication as a topic at team meetings. Open and honest discussion about communication failures can be a valuable learning point for everyone. Starting points could be:

- Design a short questionnaire based on the questions above.

- Ask someone in your team to carry out some research into communicating effectively and present it to the team.

- Ask for communication failures which the team can analyse.

It can also give valuable information about the current culture in your team. For example, if your team can engage constructively in the suggested exercises, then it indicates an open and supportive culture. If you dismiss the idea, then ask yourself why.

Tip

The Learning Made Simple book *Teams* can help you to build and maintain relationships within your team.

Making time to listen

Nature gave us one tongue and two ears so we could hear twice as much as we speak.

Epictetus

Listening to people sends a clear message that:

◆ You value their ideas and opinions, and

◆ You are interested in what they have to say.

Most people would agree that it feels good to be listened to. If your team members know you are good at listening then you will automatically lay the foundations for good performance management.

Activity

Think of someone whom you consider to be a good listener:

❖ At work

❖ In your home life

How does their ability to listen well affect the relationship you have with them?

It's likely that you more easily discuss issues or concerns with people who you know will listen. You may also use them as a 'sounding board' for ideas. Listening to people in your team will set the foundations for good working relationships, instantly meeting Maslow's needs (see Chapter 2), for social interactions and to feel good about yourself.

 We can speak at approximately 180 words a minute but think at over about 1000. Therefore our brains feel they have the capacity to listen and think (about something completely different) at the same time.

How to listen

The first rule is to stop talking yourself. You can't listen and talk at the same time. This includes resisting the inclination to interrupt. THis is very tempting, especially when you think you know what the other person is going to say.

Second, focus on what the other person is saying. Again this can be difficult for a whole variety of reasons, including:

◆   Not being interested.

◆   Not placing a value on their opinions.

◆   Being busy with your own thoughts.

> Listen or your tongue will keep you deaf.
>
> American Indian proverb

Overcoming these hurdles means you can get on with the task of listening. To help you process what you hear, try:

◆   **Summarising**. This not only helps make sure you understand but also sends the clear message that you are listening. It's impossible to summarise accurately if you haven't listened.

◆   **Asking questions**. Often when you are listening to someone you will need clarification or more information to fully understand what is being said.

Activity

Use the following checklist to assess your listening skills when you next have a discussion with someone at work. Did you:

☐   Give them plenty of opportunity to speak?

☐   Focus on what they were saying rather than letting your mind wander?

☐   Ask questions?

☐   Summarise or reflect back what they had said?

☐   Build on what they said rather than introduce your own perspective?

☐   Leave them feeling that you had actually listened?

Listening well is a skill that often needs working on. Few people will listen well on every occasion. What's important is that you build a reputation for:

1   Being able to listen

2   Making time to listen.

 If you're introducing communication onto the team agenda, don't forget to add listening. Almost everyone has the capacity to improve their listening skills!

Recognising achievements

Do you like your achievements and successes to be recognised? The chances are that you do. Being recognised by other people for our efforts and achievements tends to makes us feel good about ourselves, and this is a basic human need. Receiving recognition or praise for what we do from other people is very important in meeting that need.

How it works in practice

Recognising achievements will have a positive effect on motivation.

Boosting confidence

I had been working in HR as a recruitment officer and had the opportunity to take a secondment to deliver internal training. The first course I delivered was about recruitment and selection so although it was nerve-wracking beforehand I felt it went well. The next course was report writing. To be honest I was dreading it. On the morning of my course my manager showed me a couple of the feedback sheets from the recruitment course which commented really positively on my training skills and she told me how well I was doing to get feedback like that after my first course. It gave me a real boost and raised my confidence no end.

That was pretty typical of my manager. She seems to be able to make the team feel good about themselves.

HR officer – NHS Trust

If you don't give praise where praise is due, it will have negative impact.

Target-driven

A team leader in a call centre was under tremendous pressure to achieve sales targets. At weekly team meetings he displayed the week's results on a bar chart, comparing actuals with targets. Each week actuals were less than the targets and so he exhorted his team to try harder – more calls taking less time. After two months in the job Wayne began to allow these exhortations to go over his head. He'd tried, and although his figures had improved over the first few weeks they still weren't good enough. As long as he could keep ticking along, Wayne couldn't see anyone really getting bothered.

Giving positive feedback

Spend time thinking:

◆ Should it be given in private or in front of others? You need to think of the impact on other team members as well as the person themselves.

◆ Should you set time aside or should it be a passing comment? The formality of making time to acknowledge effort or outcomes can add to the value of the feedback.

◆ Are you making clear what it's for? If not, there's a danger that the person won't know, which in turn dilutes its impact. Also it may seem superficial. 'That was a good job' may be appropriate at times. However, giving the detail of exactly what was done to make you conclude it was done well will increase the value of the feedback.

◆ Is it sincere? Giving praise because it's a 'good thing' to do will instantly be recognised as insincere and probably patronising.

Chapter 3 looked at the skills of giving constructive feedback on performance.

Receiving feedback

Make sure that you're receptive to feedback from others:

◆ Always listen – although as the previous section highlights, this isn't always easy

◆ Don't be defensive. Be prepared to put yourself in the other person's shoes and see things from their perspective

- Thank them for the feedback, it will have given you a valuable input to learn from.

- Reflect on the feedback so you can learn from it. Understanding why someone is giving negative feedback is sometimes as important as the feedback itself.

Other ways to recognise achievement

Other ways of recognising achievement, which should be used in addition to a verbal acknowledgement could include:

- The whole team leaving early on a Friday afternoon.

- Employee of the week or month status. In some organisations this can lead to special privileges such as using a parking space close to the front entrance for a period of time.

- Taking in cakes or sweets to celebrate success.

Some of these ideas may not be appropriate due to the culture of your organisation; others may be beyond your authority to use.

Activity

Consider each person in your team individually. When was the last time you:

- ❖ Formally gave praise, e.g. in a work review or annual appraisal?

- ❖ Informally gave praise?

Now consider your team:

- ❖ When was the last time you celebrated success as a team?

If you struggle to answer then you need to plan to make the time to identify and acknowledge effort and achievement in your team.

Developing trust

People need to feel secure. They need to know they can admit mistakes, ask for help and have their 'best interests' looked after. Creating a culture of trust is much more likely to result in improved performance than a culture where everyone is 'minding their own back'.

Being trustworthy

The starting point has to be to show trustworthy behaviour yourself. Having a reputation for being trustworthy is something which usually has to be earned. It means:

◆ Not betraying confidences.

◆ Not gossiping.

◆ Considering another person's interests as well as your own.

◆ Not saying things about someone which you wouldn't say directly to them.

◆ Not taking advantage of a person's vulnerabilities.

You don't have to like a person to be trust them. Conversely you don't always trust everyone you like.

Activity

Consider your behaviour in relation to each member of your team. Can they trust you to:

☐ Keep confidences?

☐ Not discuss them with other people in the team?

☐ To keep your views on their performance private?

☐ To speak up for them when their interests are at stake?

☐ To give them honest feedback about their performance?

It's easy to think of your behaviour in terms of what you generally do. Here it's important to consider specifics as one slip can have a lasting detrimental effect on a relationship.

Building trust

In general trust develops over time. Few people will trust someone else completely at the start of any relationship but we have to start somewhere.

Activity

Supposing you have recently been recruited to a new post. You sit down with your manager to review the first few weeks and plan the work ahead.

What expectations would you have of your new manager which, if met, would begin to build trust?

Everyone's expectations will vary but it's likely to include:

◆ Following up on any promises or agreements

◆ Keeping things confidential

◆ Agreeing how you can be best supported.

If you found that your expectations were met, trust would begin to become a factor in the relationship. Usually trust has to built over time, with most people tentatively testing out whether someone can be trusted before trusting them on what they perceive as being really important matters.

Trust is two-way

Trust tends to grow by a two-way process.

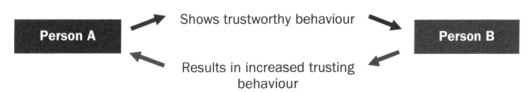

Person A — Shows trustworthy behaviour → Person B — Results in increased trusting behaviour

What expectations do you have of your team which will build a climate of trust?

It's likely to be things like:

◆ Let you know when something is going wrong.

◆ Get on with their job with minimum or no supervision.

◆ Keep to agreements.

◆ Keep confidences within the team.

Take note

You can choose who you trust, but there are no excuses for not showing trustworthy behaviour.

And when trust is a problem

A climate of mistrust is a problem. If it exists it will take a lot of work, over time, to rebuild. It needs:

◆ Recognising.

◆ Acknowledging.

◆ Agreeing a way forward.

Allocating work

Each job comes with its role and responsibilities. In the main, people are recruited for their ability to do the job, but there are likely to be times when your team has to take on new tasks or focus on new objectives. You then have to decide, who does what. The way you make and convey your decision will impact on the environment you create.

Review your current approach

Activity

Think of the last time you had to decide who did what in your team. What approach did you take to allocating work?

It's tempting to go for the option that presents least risk, i.e. choose the person who you know has the ability and will do a good job.

Adair on leadership

John Adair, management guru specialising in exploring the art of leadership identifies three team needs:

- The need to work towards common objectives.
- The need for the individual to be nurtured.
- The need for the team bonds to be nurtured.

An effective leader achieves a high performing team by catering for all these needs.

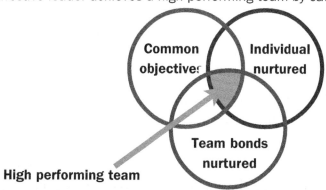

In Adair's terms this would be seen as focusing on the task at the expense of other needs in the team. Careful consideration should not only be given to the requirements of the job but also to:

◆ The current abilities and workloads of your team members;

◆ Any potential it might offer as a development opportunity.

The requirements of the job

From the outset you need to be clear about what the job, or task, involves. Key questions to ask include:

◆ What are its objectives and/or performance measures?

◆ How urgent is it?/When does it have to be done by?

◆ When could it be started?

◆ What skills and knowledge are needed to do it?

The current abilities and workload of your team members

This is about knowing your team. Through regular one-to-one meetings you'll know the capabilities and workloads of each person as well as knowing any additional pressures or stresses. This takes time, but there are no short cuts when it comes to building the sorts of relationships which will result in high performance.

Potential as a development activity

In some cases a task will be new to everybody in the team, so someone will have to learn to do it. Some demand specialist knowledge and training, which not every member of the team will have. However, there are likely to be times when you have the option of deliberately allocating the task to a member of staff as a development opportunity.

There are lots of advantages of having a ethos where development is encouraged and supported. Things to consider include:

◆ Is there time to use it as a development activity? Some jobs need to be done as quickly as possible and there is no time to do anything other than select the most appropriate person.

♦ Who will provide support? It may be you or another member of the team. Whoever it is, they must have the skills to ensure that the support is effective.

Be transparent about who you select. Tell your team why a certain piece of work has been allocated or why it's being used as a development activity. It saves misunderstandings emerging and gives people a chance to input their views – just in case you missed something.

Developing job roles

Choose a job you love, and you will never have to work a day in your life.
Confucius

Confucius was right. If you enjoy what you are doing it doesn't seem like work. You will also be prepared to put more into it because you enjoy it. In other words, it will increase your motivation. Therefore look for ways that you can let job roles evolve. As business objectives change there can often be scope for aligning job description with new directions. If not, look for ways you could rotate responsibilities or develop people to have greater flexibility in the skills they offer.

Summary

♦ To get the best out of people you have to create a culture which is motivating to work in.

♦ Your behaviour will have the biggest influence on the culture of your team.

♦ Being an effective communicator prevents a lot of problems. Check how your communication skills are perceived by your team. Improve them if necessary.

♦ Make time to listen; it sends people a clear message that they are valued.

♦ Recognise achievements and successes. If something has gone well – say so.

♦ Always show trustworthy behaviour. You don't have to trust others but they should be able to trust you.

♦ Think about the roles and responsibilities of the people you manage. Are there ways you could improve the content of their jobs?

6 Poor performance

Dealing with poor performance

Poor performance has to be acknowledged and dealt with. It often involves some form of challenging behaviour which can come in a whole range of guises. Even if you follow all the 'good practice' suggested so far, there are people who:

♦ **Won't perform** – due to low motivation or problems with their attitude.

♦ **Can't perform** – due to lack of skills, knowledge, experience, confidence, personal circumstances or even lack of resources.

Whatever the reason, you have to take action. It is highly unlikely that it will improve without intervention. In practice it will usually escalate if not dealt with.

Since banning biscuits at tea-break to improve performance, staff fitness and energy levels soared... as everyone now ran to the corner shop and back twice every day for their sugar fix.

This chapter looks at the practicalities of dealing with poor performance from two perspectives:

Understanding behaviour
• Dealing with difficult attitudes
• Recognising your response to difficult behaviour

Implementing the right processes
• Under -performance – what to do
• Taking disciplinary action

Dealing with poor performance

Dealing with difficult attitudes

People can present a whole range of difficult attitudes which cause barriers to managing their performance. They may almost be saying:

◆ I don't rate your opinion.

◆ I think I could do your job better.

◆ I do the basic minimum – don't expect any more.

◆ One word out of line and I'm looking to take a discrimination case.

It makes managing their performance very challenging. Typically, managers go into 'fight' or 'flight' mode by becoming either aggressive or taking no action and allowing the situation to escalate.

Check your inner dialogue

If someone you have to manage has a difficult attitude, first you need to check your inner dialogue, i.e. what are sorts of feelings does it cause you to have.

Activity

Below are a number of rights and responsibilities. Consider each one and decide if it applies.

☐ You have a right to manage performance.

☐ You have a right to set the agenda for a meeting.

☐ You have a right to be listened to.

You have a responsibility:

☐ To listen to the other person so that you fully understand their viewpoint

☐ To be fair and objective.

☐ To prepare thoroughly for the meeting.

They all apply to anyone whose role includes managing performance.

Tip

If you put yourself in the shoes of a member of your team, you will see that your rights become their responsibilities and your responsibilities are their rights. For example, they have a responsibility to have their performance managed, etc.

There may be occasions when you have to take someone who is being difficult back to the basics of their rights and responsibilities.

Rights when having your performance managed	Responsibilities when having your performance managed
☐ To be listened to ☐ To have fair and objective feedback ☐ To have objectives set which meet the SMART criteria	☐ To listen ☐ To follow the processes for managing performance used by your organisation

Get to know your natural response

Everyone brings their own unique personality to dealing with difficult situations. As human beings we were conditioned long ago to survive by taking a 'fight or flight' response. It's our body's primitive, inborn response for dealing with perceived attacks, harm or threats to our survival. Translated into dealing with difficult situations, it means that most managers' natural tendency is to try to ignore the behaviour or deal with it aggressively.

Responding in a logical 'adult' manner is a skill that, for most people, has to be learned.

How people deal with conflict

Research has shown that there are four main ways in which people instinctively deal with conflict at work. The response you tend to choose depends on a combination of:

◆ How concerned you are about the quality of the relationship with the other person.

◆ How concerned you are about getting a good result.

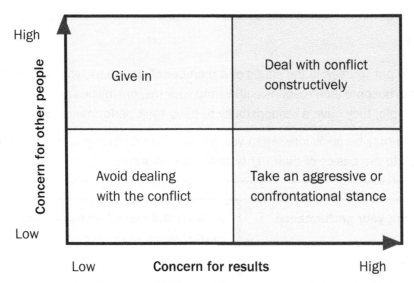

Figure 6.1 Dealing with conflict (Adapted from Thomas and Kilman model)

To understand how the different responses to conflict, work in practice, consider the scenario below.

Activity

You are just about to go home for the evening when someone comes into the office and needs your help to get a report ready for the next day. You don't particularly like the person but know that getting the report out is important.

What might you do?

There are a number of alternatives. For example:

You could.....	If so, you'd be:
Make a swift exit – if you knew you were about to be asked	... avoiding the conflict
Grit your teeth and do it under sufferance	...giving in (but possibly feeling resentful)
Say that there was 'no way' you could help	...responding aggressively
Discuss the situation and agree the most appropriate help you could give	... working together to resolve the conflict

You can probably think of occasions when you have used each approach. That's because none of them are wrong; it just depends on the circumstances.

Know yourself!

Get to know how you naturally respond to situations. Self-awareness is often the first step in being able to control your behaviour and adapt your response.

Don't make assumptions

Don't make assumptions or jump to conclusions. It's easy for the 'horns' effect to get in the way of you being objective about people, i.e. just because you rate a person because of 'X' to then assume that must also be the same with 'Y'.

Making assumptions makes an **ass** out of u and **me**! (**ass**u**me**)!

Adapting your behaviour

This is about working to resolve potential difficult situations by recognising that:

1 Other people's behaviour is a reaction to the way you behave.

2 By changing your own behaviour you can change another person's response.

It results in you taking control and influencing the situation by altering your approach.

The following scenario illustrates this at the most basic level.

Figures please, now

Nina needed some figures from Tom. Tom had said he'd get them done for the end of the day:

Nina: Tom can you give me those figures please.

Tom: No way. I've been frantic all day. You'll have to wait till tomorrow.

Nina: Oh that's great. What am I supposed to do then?

Tom: Look it's not my fault...

And so on....

You can see how the situation could escalate. Both Nina and Tom were feeding off each other's reaction and heightening the tension. Something along the lines of: 'I can see you've had a lot on. However, I've got a deadline of 10 o'clock tomorrow. Can we find a way round it?' may have helped. No guarantees of course, when you're trying to predict human behaviour.

Therefore when you are in a conflict situation it's worth asking yourself: 'What can I do differently which will cause the other person to start behaving differently?'

Assert yourself positively

Being assertive can result in other people responding positively to you. It involves:

◆ Expressing your needs/opinions/feelings in a direct and honest way.

◆ Standing up for your rights, e.g. the right to manage performance, in a way that isn't aggressive.

Tip

It you want to adapt your behaviour in difficult situations, identify someone to support you. Talking it through and identifying different approaches can be very helpful. Changing your natural response to a situation is not easy – but it is possible.

Your response to difficult behaviour

In the 1960s the psychologist Eric Berne developed a structure for analysing what can happen when people talk. Known as 'transactional analysis', it can give a useful framework for understanding why conversations between adults can be problematic. It also clearly illustrates the concept of how you, by taking control, can influence the outcome of a conversation.

Ego states

Berne identified three main 'ego states': adult, parent and child.

Talking in an *adult* state is about being objective and rational. However Berne argues that everyone is equally capable of taking on the state of 'parent' or a 'child' depending on their state of mind and the social interaction they are in.

In your *parent* state you will respond in a similar way to how your parents responded to you as a child. It may be as a nurturing parent taking on a protective role or as a critical parent, tutting at the antics of a child. In your *child* state you will either behave with natural spontaneity or in the manner you used as a child when responding to your parents. This can vary to include modifying your behaviour to conform with what your parents wanted, whining, withdrawing or rebelling. Berne called this the 'adapted child'.

Berne contends that all three states have their place in normal adult behaviour as certain triggers and situations will cause us to take on the parent and child states. Therefore constantly operating in the adult state shouldn't be seen as the ideal to aspire to.

 You can take on any of the ego states. Becoming aware what's happening when you talk to someone gives you the potential to change your own ego state and hence influence the reaction of the other person.

Ego states in the workplace

Interactions between people in the workplace demand that, for most of the time, adults interact in their adult state.

Activity

Can you identify situations when you take, with another adult, the state of:

❖ Nurturing parent

❖ Critical parent

❖ Adapted child

Most people can. Recognition of these 'states' simply provides a useful framework for:

◆ Reflecting on behaviour, and

◆ Developing a greater awareness of the effect you have on other people.

Adult – adult transactions

Generally, interactions between adults in the workplace take place on an adult-to-adult basis and the child and parent states remain hidden.

Not meeting expectations

Janice had agreed with her line manger to have a report ready by the end of the day. At two o'clock she rings her line manager. The dialogue goes:

Janice: Peter, I'm sorry but the report won't be ready for five. I've just had a call from external communications and they need me to brief them on the latest campaign urgently.

Peter: Thanks for letting me know Janice. I have to submit the findings by close of play tomorrow so things are getting really urgent. Can we meet up after you come back and plan a way forward?

Janice: No problem. I should be finished by five at the latest but are you OK to stay on if it's later?

A problem has occurred but because the two parties concerned discuss it in a rational and logical manner and it seems well on its way to be resolved.

Problem transactions

If either Janice or Peter, for whatever reason, had used a different ego state then the outcome could have been very different.

Supposing Janice's response had been as follows.

Janice: Look Peter, I can't get this report done. I'm up to my eyes already and now I've got to go and sort out external communications. You'll have to get someone else to do it or do it yourself.

In Berne's terminology, which ego state would she be taking on?

Using Berne's terminology Janice is taking on the ego state of an *adapted child*. Her line manager must then decide whether to respond in the adult state or allow the conversation to degenerate by responding as a child, for example:

'Janice, you're not the only one up to your eyes. But now I'll have my manager creating mayhem when it's not on his desk by tomorrow ...'

Or, taking on the role of critical parent Peter may have responded with:

'Oh Janice, this always seems to happen. You've let me down again. What am I supposed to do now? ...'

However, had Peter resisted his instinct to respond with either the parent or child ego, he would have increased the likelihood of the situation being resolved in a way which met his needs.

Of course, there are no guarantees, but Janice may have responded positively. The one certainty is that if Peter had succumbed to his parent or child ego state, then the chances of a satisfactory outcome would have diminished rapidly.

If you use an adult ego state then the chances are that other people will respond in an adult manner. However for a whole variety of reasons people take on either a parent or child role in either initiating or responding to each other.

Control your behaviour

You have control over your behaviour. Through your behaviour you can influence the behaviour of the people around you. Try to understand the impact of your behaviour and take control of it. In other words, when it comes to dealing with difficult people, the ball's in your court!

Using Berne's theory

Even a superficial knowledge of Berne's work can give you some insight into the behaviour of others around you. It enables you to:

◆ Understand your own triggers for taking on the parent or child roles, and

◆ Identify these roles in others, and respond accordingly.

Activity

Ask yourself:

❖ Do I interact with people using my adult ego state, all of the time or just some of the time? What makes me use other states?

❖ How do I respond to a team member using the 'child ego state'?.

❖ Do I use different state with different team members. Is this a result of how they're behaving?

Try out different behaviours, reflecting and learning from the results. Becoming more aware of the effect your behaviour has on others is key to success in the workplace as well as in relation to influencing motivation in your team. Give it thought. Don't blame others. It may be tempting to think, 'If only they would ...' but in practice it gets you nowhere.

Under-performance – what to do

Fewer than one in four civil servants thinks poor performance is dealt with effectively in their department according to an internal Whitehall survey conducted by the Institute for Public Policy Research, the leading independent think tank.

The reasons for most under-performance fall into three categories:

◆ **Ability to do the job** – have people go the right skills, knowledge or experience to do what is required of them

◆ **Behaviour and attitude** – is there something problematic with the 'mindset' of the person? e.g. are there problems with motivation; is there an attitude problem?

◆ **Personal issues** – are there personal issues which are affecting performance (e.g. health issues, relationship issues).

> Find out your organisation's policies and procedures in relation to under-performance. It is essential that you follow them, getting advice from the Human Resources department as appropriate.

The actions to take

There are likely to be five main steps you need to take.

1 Investigate

Don't ignore the situation and hope it will resolve itself. You need to find out, without being too intrusive, what's causing the under-performance. In other words, arrange a one-to-one to discuss the issue.

2 Make expectations clear

This is about being clear about what you do and don't want. Make sure you know:

◆ What satisfactory performance looks like. This could be in the form of objectives, performance measures or competencies.

◆ Why this person's performance is not satisfactory – exactly what is happening/has happened. It's about being specific.

For example, 'Your work has not been up to scratch recently' is vague and too general. Identifying specific instances sets the scene for a more productive discussion. For example, 'Last week I noticed that you didn't get the report finished on time and customer services have just contacted me to say they can't get you to respond to their queries and was anything the matter. I think we need to discuss what's happening and how we can resolve it.'

3 Check objectives are realistic

Even though you may have followed best practice in setting SMART objectives or performance measures, check that they are realistic and unforeseen factors aren't intruding.

4 Check capability

It's human nature to put off doing something we feel we can't do. Check that the person has got:

◆ The necessary skills and knowledge.

◆ The necessary resources.

If not, then update their personal development plan.

Chapter 4 looks at identifying development needs.

5 Agree a personal improvement plan

If someone has under-performed than in most cases a structured action plan for improvement is needed. Your organisation may have a standard form. If not you should include:

◆ Reason for concerns.

◆ Actions required and timescale.

◆ Development agreed.

◆ How improvement will be measured.

◆ The outcome.

 Schedule in regular one-to-ones to review progress. Be supportive. The objective is to get the person back to performing at a satisfactory level.

Taking disciplinary action

Every organisation needs a procedure for dealing with poor performance. It's usually referred to as the 'disciplinary and grievance procedure' and will cover situations where under-performance is an issue. Most procedures have a number of stages which include:

◆ An oral warning

◆ Written warning(s)

◆ Ultimately, dismissal.

There will be some types of misconduct which could lead directly to dismissal. However, in the case of under-performance, it usually starts with an oral warning and goes through written warnings. If nothing improves it can then lead to dismissal.

Before taking disciplinary action

Before you move into taking formal disciplinary action, check that:

◆ You have followed the processes put in place by your organisation to manage performance (e.g. annual appraisal meetings, regular one-to-ones).

◆ You have made available the right level of training and support.

◆ The right level of supervision has been in place.

◆ You have kept a record of all discussions in relation to under-performance.

Activity

Read your organisation's disciplinary procedure.

What specific responsibilities does it give line managers?

Summary

◆ Poor performance has to be acknowledged and dealt with. It is unlikely to improve without intervention.

◆ As a manager, you have a right and a responsibility to deal with under-performance.

◆ Getting to understand how you respond to challenging behaviour in other people can help you plan your response.

◆ People react to other people's behaviour. A change in your behaviour can change their reaction.

◆ Eric Berne identified different 'ego-states'. Recognising the different states in yourself and others can help you respond appropriately to a range of situations.

◆ Always follow your organisation's policies and procedures when you have to deal with under-performance.

Keep records

Make records of all discussions around performance. First, because it's good practice and second because they will provide evidence in any disciplinary action.

Managing performance: review

Just how well do you manage performance? Below are a series of questions. Assess your knowledge or performance against each one. For the performance-related questions, identify specific actions which demonstrate how you met each one. If, on reflection, you feel you need to do something else, or differently, then transfer it to your Personal Development Plan.

Knowledge

Understanding the wider context

Do you know:

- ☐ the main changes in your organisation over the last two years?
- ☐ What has driven these changes?
- ☐ What are the changes which are likely to happen in the next two years?
- ☐ What's driving them?
- ☐ Does your organisation have a mission, vision or values? If so what are they?
- ☐ What are your organisation's strategic/business objectives
- ☐ What is the business planning cycle for your organisation?
- ☐ What are the objectives for your area of the organisation?

The performance management system in your organisation

Do you know the policies and procedures relating to:

- ☐ Managing performance?
- ☐ Development?
- ☐ Under-performance?
- ☐ Taking disciplinary action?

Theories relating to how people operate in the workplace

Do you have some knowledge of:

☐   Maslow's hierarchy of satisfaction?

☐   Herzberg's satisfiers and motivators?

☐   Expectancy theory?

☐   Berne's ego-states?

Your performance

Can you give a specific examples of how you have managed performance by:

☐   Systematically assessing performance prior to a one-to-one?

☐   Giving constructive feedback?

☐   Setting SMART objectives?

☐   Identifying development needs?

☐   Supporting the transfer of learning to the workplace?

☐   Can you give examples of actions you have taken to create a culture which is maximising your team's performance?

☐   Can you give examples of what actions you have taken to deal with someone who was under-performing?

Index

For Product Safety Concerns and Information please contact our EU
representative GPSR@taylorandfrancis.com Taylor & Francis Verlag GmbH,
Kaufingerstraße 24, 80331 München, Germany

Printed and bound by CPI Group (UK) Ltd, Croydon, CR0 4YY
08/06/2025
01897003-0020